Reading & Writing TARGETS 2

Student's Book

Virginia Evans - Jenny Dooley

Express Publishing

Published by Express Publishing

Liberty House, New Greenham Park, Newbury,
Berkshire RG19 6HW
Tel.: (0044) 1635 817 363
Fax: (0044) 1635 817 463
e-mail: inquiries@expresspublishing.co.uk
http://www.expresspublishing.co.uk

© Jenny Dooley - Virginia Evans, 1998

Design & Illustration © Express Publishing, 1998

First published 1998
New edition 2000
Sixth impression 2007

Made in EU

ISBN 978-1-903128-84-8

Acknowledgements

Authors' Acknowledgements

We would like to thank all the staff at Express Publishing who have contributed their skills to producing this book. Thanks are due in particular to the following for their support and patience: Mary Palmer (editor in chief); Steve Ladd (senior editor); Rebecca Yates and Richard Howell (editorial assistants); Philippa Porter (senior production controller); E. Mavragani (art director), Helen Mavrodemos (assistant designer) and our design team; Tasso Sinerli (artist); and Julie Brown Lucy Whetman, Janet Phillips, Mary Lewis, Annette Pearson, Debbie Ellis and M. Rowell. We would also like to thank those institutions and teachers who piloted the manuscript, and whose comments and feedback influenced positively the production of the book.

Photograph Acknowledgements

Audio Visual for photographs on pages 36 (top right © 1985 by MGM/VA Entertainment Co. All rights reserved), 37 (top left © 1985 by MGM/VA Entertainment Co. All rights reserved), 39.

Contents

New Friends...

1.....................

2.....................

3.....................

4.....................

5.....................

1 These are photographs of Isabel Garcia's family. a) Read the letter below and write the names of the people in the photographs. b) Answer these questions about the letter.

- How does the letter start?
- How does the letter finish?
- Which of these phrases can you use to start a letter to a friend?
  a) Dear John, b) Dear Mr Smith, c) Dear Sirs,
- Which of these phrases can you use to finish a letter to a friend?
  a) Best wishes, b) Yours sincerely, c) Love and kisses, d) Love,

2 Read the letter that Isabel sent to her new pen-friend again, then read the sentences (1-5) and underline the correct words.

25, Plaza de Toros
Granada
Spain
10th September, 19 ... .

Dear Hasan,

Hello! My name is Isabel Garcia and I am your new pen-friend. I am fourteen years old and I am Spanish. I live in Granada in Spain.

These are photographs of the people in my family. My father's name is Philip. He's a chemist. My mother's name is Marcia. My brother's name is Fredrico and my sister's name is Rosa. I am the girl with short brown hair. My dog's name is Pluto. He's in the photograph with me.

I like tennis but I don't like basketball. My favourite subject is Geography, but I don't like Chemistry because it's difficult. I love pop music but I don't like opera. I like dogs but I don't like cats. My favourite singer is Elton John and my favourite actress is Melanie Griffith. They are fantastic!

What about you? What do you like? Who is your favourite singer? Please write soon and tell me about yourself.

Best wishes,
Isabel

1 Isabel is from **Spain/Mexico.**
2 Her father's name is **Philip/ Fredrico.**
3 Her sister's name is **Marcia/Rosa.**
4 Her favourite subject is **Chemistry/ Geography.**
5 Isabel doesn't like **cats/dogs.**

3 Match the phrases from the letter with the correct photographs.

A I like dogs but I don't like cats.
B I like tennis but I don't like basketball.
C My favourite subject is geography.
D My favourite actress is Melanie Griffith.

1 ....

2 .... 3 .... 4 ....

4 Match the pictures with the jobs in the list, then explain what the other jobs are.

teacher, hairdresser, waiter, actor, doctor, vet, builder, baker, postman, firefighter

b .... c ....
a ....
d ....
f ....
e ....

STUDY TIP

Singular & Plural Nouns

nationality	➡	nationalities
brother	➡	brothers
motorbike	➡	motorbikes
piano	➡	pianos

5 Write the plurals for these nouns.

1 family = ... 5 singer = ...
2 sister = ... 6 city = ...
3 horse = ... 7 actor = ...
4 disco = ... 8 subject = ...

6 Read the letter from Ex. 2 again and complete the table below. Then, look at your notes and talk about Isabel Garcia.

Start like this: *Isabel Garcia is 14 years old. She is Spanish. She lives ...*

Name:	*Isabel Garcia*
Age:	....
Nationality:	....
Address:	.........., ..., ..., ...
Family:	*father - Philip - chemist*
	mother - ....
	brother - ....
	.... - Rosa
Pets:	.... - ....
Likes:	........, ..., ..., ..., ..., ...,
Dislikes:	........, ..., ..., ...

7 Look at the notes in Ex. 6, then write answers to the questions, as in the examples.

• Does Isabel like Geography? *Yes, she does.*
• Does she like Chemistry? *No, she doesn't.*
• Does she like football? *I don't know.*

1 Does she like dogs? ....
2 Does she like cats? ....
3 Does she like Granada? ....
4 Does she like Elton John? ....

8 Match the opposites in the list with the adjectives below.

new, fantastic, tasteless, big, boring, tiring, difficult, safe

1 easy ≠ .... 5 small ≠ ....
2 horrible ≠ .... 6 delicious ≠ ....
3 interesting ≠ .... 7 relaxing ≠ ....
4 old ≠ .... 8 dangerous ≠ ....

5

9 Study the examples below, then fill in the gaps with *but, because* or *and.*

I like dogs **but** I don't like cats.
I don't like Chemistry **because** it's difficult.
I am fourteen years old **and** I am Spanish.

1 I like dogs .... horses.
2 My favourite subject is Geography .... it's easy.
3 Lucy lives in Spain .... she isn't Spanish.
4 I like skateboarding .... swimming.
5 I like Antonio Banderas .... he's a fantastic actor.

10 Match the pictures with the activities in the list.

swimming, playing tennis, dancing, watching TV, reading, painting, fishing, eating pizza, listening to music, going to the cinema

11 **ABOUT YOU**
Use the following adjectives to say what you like and don't like, giving reasons as in the example. You may use the activities listed in Ex. 10 as well as your own ideas.

difficult, fantastic, easy, boring, delicious, relaxing

e.g. **I don't like** watching TV **because** it's boring.
I like eating pizzas **because** they are delicious.

12 **COUNTRIES AND NATIONALITIES**
Fill in the table below, then use the words to write sentences, as in the example.

NAME:	COUNTRY:	NATIONALITY:
Abdul	Egypt	....
Carla	....	Italian
Miguel	....	Mexican
Murat	Turkey	....
Diana	Britain	....
Paola	....	Brazilian
Dimitri	Greece	....
Marak	Poland	....

1 *My name's Abdul. I'm from Egypt. I'm Egyptian.*
2 ....
3 ....
4 ....
5 ....
6 ....
7 ....
8 ....

13 Look at the map and complete the sentences.

KEY
● = city
■ = town
◆ = village

SCOTLAND
● Glasgow
◆ Hamilton

WALES   ENGLAND
◆ Congleton
Swansea
● Birmingham

1 *Birmingham is a city in England.*
2 Swansea .... Wales.
3 Hamilton .... Scotland.
4 Congleton ....
5 Glasgow ....

Apostrophe (')

My name**'s** Helen. (**'s = is**)

My brother**'s** name is John. (**possessive: His** name is John.)

I like cat**s**. (**no apostrophe – plural**)

14 Fill in the short forms.

Long forms	Short forms	Long forms	Short forms
I am=	I'm	It is =	....
You are=	....	We are =	....
He is=	....	You are =	....
She is=	....	They are =	....

15 Read the paragraph below and put apostrophes in the right places.

My names Helen. I am your new pen-friend. My fathers name is Richard. Hes a teacher. My mothers name is Sarah and shes a nurse. I like dancing. My favourite subject is Maths. Its easy!

Note: You can use both short and long forms in letters to friends.

16 Complete the form with information about yourself.

Pen-friends International
Name:
Age:
Nationality:
Address:
Family:
Pets:
Likes:
Dislikes:

WRITING

When you write a letter to a new pen-friend, write your address and the date in the top right-hand corner. Start your letter with **Dear** + **your pen-friend's first name**, and finish with **Best wishes,** + **your first name**. Always divide your letter into paragraphs.

17 Choose one of these people as your new pen-friend, then use the plan below and write a letter to him/her. Use the letter from Ex. 2 as a model.

Name: Sam Walker
Age: 12
Nationality: British

Name: Lisa Rosi
Age: 16
Nationality: Italian

Plan

(your address)
....
....
....
....
(date)..................

Dear *(your pen-friend's first name)*,

Paragraph 1: *greetings - introduce yourself (name, age, nationality, where you live...)*
↓
Paragraph 2: *family and pets*
↓
Paragraph 3: *likes and dislikes*
↓
Paragraph 4: *end your letter (Please write soon ...)*

Best wishes,

(your first name)
....

From Monday to Friday ...

BRAVO

FOR YOUNG PEOPLE AROUND THE WORLD!

This week ...
✓ What do you do every day?
✓ What is your favourite day?

INSIDE:
An Oxford teenager's typical day

1 Look at the cover of the magazine and answer the questions below.

- What is the name of the magazine?
- Who is it for?
- What is the article inside the magazine about?
- How old is a *teenager*?
- Can you say the names of the days in English?
- What is the day today? Is it your favourite day? Why?Why not?

2 Read the article which Melanie wrote about her daily routine for *Bravo* magazine, then read the statements and mark them as true (**T**) or false (**F**).

An Oxford teenager's typical day

My Day!

My name is Melanie Smith. I'm sixteen years old and I live in Oxford in England. From Monday to Friday my daily routine is always the same.

My day always starts at eight o'clock in the morning when I get up and have a shower. Then I go downstairs and have a quick breakfast with my family. I usually have toast and a glass of milk, but I never have bacon and eggs. After breakfast I make my bed and then I go to school.

I stay at school from nine o'clock in the morning until half past three in the afternoon. On Tuesdays and Thursdays I stay later because I have guitar lessons. On the other days I usually go shopping with my friends. When I get home I often take our dog, Gemma, for a walk.

I always do my homework from five o'clock until half past six or sometimes seven o'clock in the evening. Then, we all have dinner together. After dinner, my brother and I usually do the washing-up. I often watch TV for about an hour after dinner but my brother never does. He always plays computer games in his room. He's crazy about them! If I don't watch TV, I sometimes call my friend Sally for a chat. I always go to bed before eleven o'clock.

After such a busy day, I usually feel sleepy and ready for my comfortable bed!

1 Melanie has a shower at 9 o'clock in the morning. ☐
2 She always has bacon and eggs for breakfast. ☐
3 She makes her bed before breakfast. ☐
4 She usually stays at school until half past three in the afternoon. ☐
5 She has guitar lessons on Mondays and Fridays. ☐
6 She often takes Gemma for a walk when she gets home. ☐
7 She usually does the washing-up with her brother after dinner. ☐
8 She never watches TV after dinner. ☐

STUDY TIP

Adverbs of frequency (always, never, usually, sometimes, often, etc) normally go **before** the **main verb** (e.g. *I always get up early.*) but **after auxiliary verbs** and the verb **to be** (e.g. *I don't usually have coffee for breakfast. I am never late for school.*).

3   Fill in: *do, have, go, make*. Then use the collocations to make sentences, as in the example.

1 .... shopping
2 .... a shower
3 .... breakfast

4 .... my bed
5 .... my homework
6 .... the washing-up

7 .... lunch
8 .... home
9 .... the housework

10 .... a cake
11 .... for a walk
12 .... a nap

e.g.   *I usually go shopping in the afternoon.*

4   Read the article in Ex. 2 again and underline the adverbs of frequency. Then make sentences using the notes below.
e.g. *She always gets up and has a shower at eight o'clock in the morning.*

1 She always .... and .... / 8 am.

2 Then she .... and .... / her family.

3 She .... / 9 am.

4 She usually .... / her friends on Mondays.

5 When she gets home she often .... / for a walk.

6 She always .... /5 - 6.30 or 7 pm.

7 Then she .... / her family.

8 She usually .... / dinner.

9 She often .... /about 1 hr after dinner.

10 She always .... /11 pm.

5   How often do you do the following activities? Tick the appropriate boxes in the questionnaire below.

	always	sometimes	usually	often	never
1 help with the ironing?					
2 go to the gym after school/work?					
3 eat pizza for supper?					
4 go to the cinema in the evening?					
5 invite friends home for supper?					
6 play basketball at the weekend?					
7 ride your bike to work/school?					
8 visit a museum in your free time?					

6   Now, in pairs, ask and answer questions as in the example below.

e.g.   SA: **How often** do you help with the ironing?
       SB: I **never** help with the ironing. What about you?
       SA: I **sometimes** help with the ironing. **How often** do you ...?
       SB: I **always** ...

7   • What do you always do on weekdays?
       • What do you usually do during the weekend?

8 Add the prepositions and put the words in the correct column.

the weekend, the morning, Tuesday, Wednesday afternoon, nine o'clock, Sunday morning, the evening, half past three, Monday night, the afternoon, a quarter to one, Christmas, May, Christmas Day

At	In	On
at the weekend	*in* the morning	*on* Tuesday

9 Match the opposites in the list with the adjectives below.

busy, sad, ugly, horrible, wide awake, late, bored, noisy

1 pretty ≠ ....
2 excited ≠ ....
3 early ≠ ....
4 peaceful ≠ ....

5 happy ≠ ....
6 sleepy ≠ ....
7 lazy ≠ ....
8 lovely ≠ ....

10 Read the text below and choose the correct sentence for each gap.

a People work in their gardens or wash their cars.
b I can stay at home with my family.
c I can even hear the birds in the trees.
d Cars, buses and people go past our house all day.

My family and I live on a busy main road. **1)** .... They never stop! But Sunday is a lovely day. I wake up early, and everything is peaceful. **2)** .... Sometimes I take my dog for a walk. The road looks different on Sundays. **3)** .... For me Sunday is a lazy day. **4)** .... Sunday is my favourite day of the week.

11 Complete the sentences below giving reasons, as in the example.

1 School is great on Fridays because *I have English and Geography. They are my favourite subjects.*
2 I don't like Mondays at school because ....
....
3 Ten o'clock in the evening is late for me. I usually ....
....
4 I'm always busy on Saturday mornings. I ....
....
5 Sunday is my favourite day because ....
....
6 Wednesday is a busy day for me. I often ....
....
7 Saturday afternoon is lovely because I ....
....
8 On Sunday evenings I usually feel sad because ....
....

12 Read the text about Melanie's father and fill in the correct form of the verbs in brackets.

My father always **1)** .... **(get up)** very early because he **2)** .... **(work)** as a baker. He **3)** .... **(have)** breakfast at three o'clock in the morning and then he **4)** .... **(go)** to work at half past three. He never **5)** .... **(make)** the bed because my mother always **6)** .... **(get up)** after him.

He **7)** .... **(work)** at the bakery until half past twelve, then he **8)** .... **(come)** home and **9)** .... **(have)** lunch with my mother. He **10)** .... **(go)** back to the bakery and **11)** .... **(stay)** there until six o'clock.

In the evenings my father often **12)** .... **(meet)** his friends at the pub. He sometimes **13)** .... **(stay)** at home and **14)** .... **(watch)** TV with us. He always **15)** .... **(go)** to bed at eleven o'clock.

My father's weekdays **(16)** .... **(start)** very early but he **(17)** .... **(seem)** to enjoy them!

WRITING

13 Sally, Melanie's best friend, wrote an article for *Bravo* about her favourite day of the week. Read the paragraphs below and put them in the correct order.

a. I usually go home at about seven o'clock in the evening. Sometimes I go out with my family to a restaurant for dinner or we stay at home and order food from Mario's Pizzeria. Their food is delicious! After that we usually watch TV. A lot of my favourite programmes are on Saturday night, so I often go to bed late.

b. Saturday is my favourite day of the week because I can do whatever I like. I don't go to school so I get up late in the morning. After breakfast I usually go shopping with my mum. We often go to the supermarket around the corner.

c. I'm always happy after such a lovely day and I feel really glad because the next day, Sunday, is a day off, too!

d. After that I sometimes help my mum with lunch. I usually make the salad and Mum cooks the meal. We never have lunch before one o'clock. After lunch my family and I often play Scrabble. It's our favourite game! At about five o'clock I sometimes visit my best friend, Melanie, and we listen to pop music.

14 Use the plan and the words in the list below to write an article about your daily routine for *Bravo* magazine. Use the article from Ex. 2 as a model.

in the morning/afternoon/evening, then, after that, always, sometimes, usually, often, never

Plan

Paragraph 1:	Introduce yourself ... *(name/ age/where you live)*
Paragraph 2:	In the morning ... *(get up/ have a shower/ have breakfast/ make your bed/ go to school/work, etc)*
Paragraph 3:	In the afternoon ... *(come home from school/work/ have lunch/ go shopping/ do your homework, etc)*
Paragraph 4:	In the evening ... *(have supper/ watch TV/ read magazines/ go to the cinema/ go to bed, etc)*
Paragraph 5:	How you feel at the end of the day ... *(happy/ tired/ sad/ glad, etc.)* **and reason**

A Home away from Home ...

Come to Marton-on-Sea

Choose one of our lovely, inexpensive holiday homes.

1 The following short descriptions are from a brochure with information about holiday homes. Read them and match them with the photographs.

1 Rose Villa
A beautiful, stone house next to the sea.

2 Holly Cottage
A quiet, pretty house outside the town.

3 The Marton Apartment
A comfortable apartment in the town centre.

2 Read the two passages below and decide which of the holiday homes from Ex. 1 they describe. Write the name of the holiday home in the gap, then answer the questions below.

A .... is for up to five or six people. It is near the beach and a mile from the town centre. It has got a living-room, a kitchen, three bedrooms and two bathrooms. In the living-room there is a television and a comfortable sofa. The kitchen has everything you need, with an electric cooker and a fridge. Upstairs there are three bedrooms. Each room has got two beds. The two bathrooms, one upstairs and one downstairs, have got a bath, basin and toilet. There is also a small garden. You can sit under the trees and have lunch, or you can walk from the garden to the sea in less than a minute.

B .... is for up to three people. It is near the best shops and restaurants in the town. It is one mile from the sea. It has got a large living-room with a television and a sofa, and a big fireplace. There are two bedrooms. The first bedroom is big, with a double bed. The second one is smaller, with a single bed in it. There is also a bathroom with a shower, basin and toilet. The kitchen has an electric cooker and a fridge. There is a balcony with a table and chairs where you can sit and watch the sunset. This holiday home is next to a square full of colourful flowers — they smell lovely!

1 What are the main features of each holiday home?
2 What are the special features of each holiday home?

3 Use the words from the list to label the pictures.

sofa, cooker, fridge, bath, shower, basin, double bed, single bed, wardrobe, armchair, dishwasher, fireplace

1  2

3 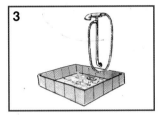 4

5  6

7  8

9  10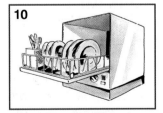

11 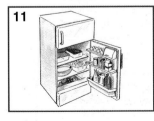 12

4 Which of the items above would you find in: a) a bedroom, b) a kitchen, c) a bathroom and d) a living-room?

5 Study the following examples and say when you use *there is/are*.

> **There is** a television in the living-room.
> **There is** a small garden outside the house.

> **There are** two bedrooms in the flat.
> **There are** some posters on the wall.

6 Read the text below from the holiday brochure and fill in *is* or *are*.

Marton-on-Sea is a lovely place for a holiday. There **1)** .... some great shops and restaurants in the town centre and there **2)** .... some lovely, quiet places outside the town. We have three super holiday homes in Marton-on-Sea. In the town centre there **3)** .... a very comfortable modern apartment. Outside the town there **4)** .... two larger houses. There **5)** .... a beautiful stone house near the sea and there **6)** .... also a quiet, pretty cottage. Choose any of the three for an unforgettable holiday!

7 Read the dialogue below in which a travel agent gives you information about Rose Villa. Then, fill in the gaps with the correct word(s).

You: Could you give me some information about Rose Villa, please?
T. Agent: Well, it's a beautiful house near the **1)** .... and a mile from the **2)** ....
You: How many people is it for?
T. Agent: It is for **3)** .... people.
You: How many rooms has it got?
T. Agent: It has got a lovely **4)** ...., a large **5)** ...., three big **6)** .... and two **7)** ....
You: Is there a television?
T. Agent: Yes, there is. There is one in the **8)** ....
You: Is there anything special about it?
T. Agent: Yes, there is. There is a small garden where you can sit under the **9)** .... and **10)** ....
You: How far is it from the sea?
T. Agent: Very close. You can walk from the **11)** .... to the **12)** .... in less than a minute.
You: Thank you very much!

8 Read the following text and fill in the correct prepositions from the list below.

behind, in, on, between, next to, above, beside, in front of

This is a picture of the beautiful modern living-room in the Marton Apartment. It has got a glass door and three big windows. There is a large fireplace **1)** .... the door and one of the windows. There are two pictures **2)** .... the fireplace and **3)** .... it there is a comfortable armchair. There is a brown rug **4)** .... the fireplace. There is a leather sofa and a glass table on the rug. There are some plants **5)** .... the sofa. **6)** .... the sofa there is a small table with an antique lamp **7)** .... it. There is also a television and a stereo **8)** .... the room. It is definitely the perfect living-room for your holiday comfort!

9 Match the adjectives in the list with their opposites below, then make sentences as in the example.

horrible, modern, ugly, expensive, small, uncomfortable, noisy, colourful

1 inexpensive ≠ ....
2 old-fashioned ≠............
3 comfortable ≠............
4 dull ≠ ....

5 large ≠ ....
6 lovely ≠ ....
7 quiet ≠ ....
8 beautiful ≠ ....

e.g. *There is an **inexpensive** hotel near a **lovely** park.*

- You can use **where** to join two sentences which describe a feature of a house.
  e.g. *There is a small garden. You can sit there.*
  *There is a small garden **where** you can sit.*

10 Join the sentences below using

1 There is a shop downstairs. You can buy flowers there.
There ....
2 There is a restaurant. You can eat delicious steaks there.
There ....
3 It has got a beach. You can sunbathe there.
It ....
4 There is a garden. You can play there.
There ....
5 There are some shops. You can buy expensive clothes there.
There ....

11 Fill in the correct verb from the list below.

sit, look, watch, have, do, park, play, eat

1 There is a table where you can ..*sit*.. and ..*eat*..
2 There are two televisions in this house, so you can .... the programmes you want.
3 This house has got two bathrooms. You can .... a bath in one or a shower in the other.
4 There is a washing-machine so you can .... all your washing.
5 There is a double garage where you can .... two cars.
6 The house has got a lovely garden where the children can ....
7 There is a veranda where you can sit and .... at the sea.

12 Look at the information about Holly Cottage and complete the dialogue below.

near the sea

3 miles from the town centre

HOLLY COTTAGE - THE BIGGEST AND BEST OF ALL OUR HOLIDAY HOMES.

A large house for up to eight people
- 4 bedrooms - with two single beds in each one
- living-room - with a TV and a comfortable sofa
- kitchen - with a cooker, a fridge and a dishwasher
- two bathrooms - one with a shower and one with a bath

Special Features!

Big garden - you can have a barbecue there

Double garage - you can park two cars there

A: Can you tell me about ...., please?
B: Well, it's the .... and the .... of all our holiday homes in Marton. It's a large ....
.... for ....
A: Where is it?
B: It's three ....
A: Is it near the sea?
B: Yes, ...
A: How many rooms are there?
B: There are four ...., a ...., a .... and two ....

13 Answer the questions about Holly Cottage.

- What is there in the living-room?
- What is there in each of the four bedrooms?
- What is there in the kitchen?
- What is there in the bathrooms?
- What are the special features of the cottage? What can you do in each of these?

WRITING

TIP

When you describe a holiday home say: a) **what kind of place it is** (cottage, flat, etc), b) **where it is**, c) **what the interior is like** (rooms, furniture, etc), d) **what special features it has got** (garage, garden, etc) *and* e) **what you can do there**. Use **adjectives** to make your description more interesting for the reader. Use *where* to link some of your sentences.

14 Look at the information about Holly Cottage in Ex. 12, then use the plan below and the picture from the Photo File section to write a description of the cottage for a holiday brochure.

Plan

Write about
- what kind of house it is
- how many people it is for
- where it is
- what the interior is like (how many rooms there are, what there is/are in each room, etc)
- what special features it has got/why they are special/what you can do there

Having a Wonderful Time...

1 Look at the pictures and match them with the descriptions below.

1 a hotel with a swimming pool ......
2 souvenirs at a market ....
3 a sunset ....
4 shells ....
5 ruins ....
6 donkeys ....
7 souvlaki ....
8 snorkelling ....

2 Read the letter and answer the questions.

Dear Rachel,

I am having a wonderful time here! We are on a lovely island in the Cyclades, called Santorini. The hotel we are staying at is nice and quiet. It's got a lovely swimming pool.

The weather is hot and sunny. Right now, I am sitting outside a fantastic café by the sea. Paul is snorkelling in the clear water, as usual. He is looking for some shells to take home. Dad is visiting some ancient ruins on the island. Dad enjoys visiting old places — I think they're boring. Mum is buying souvenirs at the market. She loves the market but it's a bit noisy for me.

We go to restaurants nearly every night for dinner. My favourite one is by the sea. Mum and Dad always order seafood but I never do — it's horrible. I order souvlaki — it's so delicious! The sunsets are spectacular and the local people are really friendly, too. I love it here so much, I never want to leave!

Oh well, that's all for now. See you next week.

Love,
Suzanne

P.S.   There are a lot of donkeys on the island. They usually carry people's bags to their hotels. They are so patient and gentle!

1 Who is the letter to?
2 Which island is Suzanne on?
3 Where is Suzanne staying?
4 What is Suzanne doing right now?
5 What is Paul doing?
6 What is Suzanne's mother doing?
7 What is Suzanne's father doing?
8 Where is her favourite restaurant?
9 What does she always order?
10 Is she enjoying her holiday?

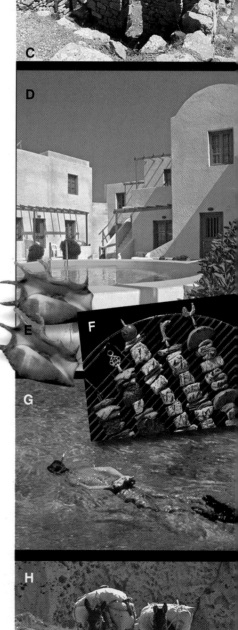

3 Match the words from the text to their definitions.

1	wonderful	a	not interesting
2	quiet	b	pieces of a very old building
3	ancient	c	peaceful
4	ruins	d	great
5	boring	e	almost
6	a bit	f	very old
7	nearly	g	awful
8	horrible	h	a little

4 Say and write which nouns go with which adjectives.

1	sky	7	town
2	beach	8	lake
3	ruins	9	café
4	cake	10	souvlaki
5	hotel	11	temple
6	sea	12	seafood

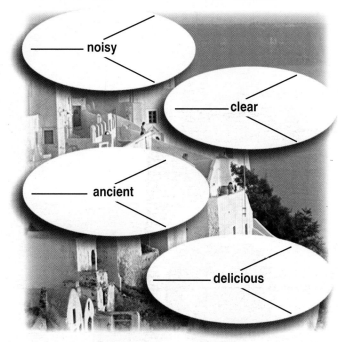

noisy

clear

ancient

delicious

5 Underline the correct verb.

1 People on holiday **visit/play in** ancient places.
2 You can go **climbing/snorkelling** in the sea.
3 People **buy/take** souvenirs at a market.
4 People **get/take** photographs of temples.
5 You can **go/do** skiing in the mountains.
6 You can **watch/look** beautiful sunsets.
7 People can **ask/order** food in a restaurant.
8 You can **stay/leave** at a hotel.

6 Read Suzanne's letter again and look at the items below. A) Find adjectives from the letter and write them beside each item.
B) Tick which ones Suzanne *likes/doesn't like*. Finally, talk about them giving reasons for her choice, as in the example.

e.g. Suzanne **likes** Santorini **because** it's **lovely**.
      She **doesn't like** ...

			likes	doesn't like
1	Santorini	*lovely*	✓	
2	The hotel	....		
3	The café by the sea	....		
4	Ancient ruins	....		
5	The market	....		
6	Seafood	....		
7	Souvlaki	....		
8	The sunsets	....		
9	The local people	....		
10	The donkeys	....		

STUDY TIP

Give a **reason** when you talk about **what you like/don't like** about your holidays. Use **adjectives** such as beautiful, fantastic, lovely, noisy, crowded, delicious, spectacular, etc.

7 Look at the key and use the notes below to say what you *like/don't like* about your holidays, giving reasons, as in the example.

e.g. I **love** eating seafood **because** it is **delicious**.

KEY:

- eating seafood
- snorkelling
- visiting ancient ruins
- watching the sunsets
- lying in the sun
- staying at seaside hotels
- writing postcards
- shopping for souvenirs
- cafés by the sea
- rainy weather

 love

like

 don't like

 hate

8 Use the correct form of the verbs in the list to fill in the part of the letter below.

ski, write, sit, learn, fall, sing

Right now I 1) .... by a lovely fire and I 2) .... to you. It's warm and friendly in here, and some people 3) .... beside the piano. Jack and I 4) .... to ski. Jack is outside now. He 5) .... Well, actually, right now he 6) .... over ...

9 A) Match the seasons with the pictures.

winter, spring, summer, autumn

B) Read the sentences under each picture and choose the one which describes it best.

a It's cold and it's snowing.
b It's wet and it's raining.

a The weather is hot, sunny and dry.
b It's cloudy, windy and wet.

a It's sunny, bright and fresh.
b The weather is icy and freezing.

a The weather is windy and foggy.
b It's hot and sunny and the sky is blue.

Study these examples.

In the north **but on** the north coast **In** the east **but on** the east coast **In** the south **but on** the south coast **In** the west **but on** the west coast

10 Look at the map of Italy and fill in the gaps below.

1 Rome is .... the .... of Italy.
2 Naples is .... the .... - .... of Italy.
3 Sicily is .... the .... of Italy.
4 Milan is .... the .... of Italy.
5 San Marino is .... the .... - .... coast of Italy.

11 Janet is on holiday in Alanya. Read her letter and fill in the topic sentences from the box. One of the sentences does not fit.

Dear Vicky,

1) ....
We are in a beautiful seaside town called Alanya. It is on the south coast of Turkey. We are staying at a small hotel near an indoor market.

2) ....
The sun is shining and it's very hot. Rob is learning to scuba-dive. Mum is visiting the indoor market. She loves shopping, but the market is too crowded for me. Dad is taking photographs of an ancient temple near our hotel. He really likes old buildings, but I think they're boring.

3) ....
It has some lovely restaurants. My favourite one has delicious fresh clams! After dinner we usually go for a walk around the town or have a cup of coffee in one of Alanya's great cafés.

4) ....

Love,
Janet

P.S. This is a picture of some shoe-shiners in front of our hotel. I like them — they're so unusual!

A	Right now, I am sitting on a beautiful beach.
B	I miss you. See you in two weeks.
C	It's raining all the time!
D	I am having a fantastic time.
E	Alanya is a wonderful place for a holiday.

WRITING

TIP

When you write a friendly letter while on holiday, write about: **where** you are, **the place** you are staying at, **the weather**, **what** you are doing, **who** you are with and **what** they are doing. Write **what you like/don't like** giving **reasons**, as well as what your **impressions** are. Use a variety of **adjectives** to make your letter more interesting.

13 Use the plan below to write a holiday letter to a friend.

Plan

Dear .....(your friend's first name),

Paragraph 1: • *where you are on holiday and where you are staying*

Paragraph 2: • *the weather*
• *what you are doing at the moment*
• *who you are with*
• *what they are doing at the moment*

Paragraph 3: • *your impressions about the place, the food and general activities*

Paragraph 4: • *close your letter (see you soon/bye for now, etc)*

Love,

....
(your first name)

12 Read Janet's letter again and underline the sentences that describe the pictures below.

Happy New Year!

1 Match the texts to the pictures. Which text does not match a picture?

A
In my country, carnival is a special occasion. People dress up in colourful costumes and dance in the streets. Everyone feels happy.

B
In my country, we celebrate Christmas on December 25th. People buy presents and decorate their houses with Christmas trees. They also eat roast turkey. Everyone feels happy and relaxed.

C
In my country, children often celebrate their birthdays with a birthday party for friends. They blow out the candles on the birthday cake and play games. Everyone feels excited.

D
In my country, July 4th is a national holiday. People watch the parades, go to the beach or have a barbecue at home. Everyone feels very proud.

E
In my country, we celebrate Id al Fitr after the fast of Ramadan. We visit all our friends and family and give each other presents. We buy new clothes and we all feel pleased because it is the end of Ramadan.

2 Which of the pictures shows a **national holiday** and which shows a **religious holiday**?

3 Read the article and answer the questions.

New Year's Eve in Scotland

by Julie MacAlistair

It's December 31st, New Year's Eve in Scotland. It's the time when the Scots celebrate the arrival of the new year.

People usually have parties in their houses. They send invitations to friends and decorate their houses with colourful balloons and banners saying "Happy New Year". They also buy drinks and prepare delicious food.

On the evening of December 31st people dress in their best clothes and go to parties. They dance, eat and have fun. When the clock strikes twelve everyone shouts "Happy New Year!" They all join hands and sing a traditional Scottish song, "Auld Lang Syne". This song tells us to forget the bad things and all be friends. Then everybody kisses each other and they all have a glass of Scotch whisky. People often set off magnificent fireworks in the streets too. Soon after midnight people visit their friends and neighbours. The first man to enter a house brings good luck with him.

New Year's Eve is wonderful. Everyone has fun and feels happy. It's a perfect way to welcome the new year.

1 Where and when does the celebration take place?
2 What do people celebrate?
3 What preparations do they make for the celebration?
4 What happens on the evening of December 31st?
5 What do they sing?
6 What does the song tell us to do?
7 How do people feel?

20

4 Read the article again and underline the adjective-noun collocations. Close your books and try to remember as many as possible.

e.g. colourful balloons

5 What do these words mean? Look at the text and choose the correct meanings.

1 *welcome* means... **a** say hello **b** say goodbye
2 *decorate* means... **a** make ugly **b** make beautiful
3 *colourful* means... **a** bright **b** dark
4 *traditional* means... **a** modern **b** historical
5 *set off* means... **a** light **b** blow
6 *banner* means... **a** flag **b** letter

6 Underline the correct word.

1 People in Scotland **celebrate/forget** the arrival of the new year on December 31st.
2 They **fix/prepare** food for the party.
3 People **join/keep** hands and sing songs on New Year's Day.
4 People **welcome/visit** friends' houses to wish them "Happy New Year".
5 When the clock **hits/strikes** twelve they all sing "Auld Lang Syne".
6 Everyone has fun and **touches/feels** happy.
7 They set off **fireworks/fires** in the evening.
8 They send **signs/invitations** for the party.

7 Fill in the missing adjectives from the list.

colourful, delicious, best, happy, traditional, magnificent, good, perfect

1 "Danny Boy" is a .... Irish song.
2 Everyone wishes each other a .... New Year at midnight on December 31st.
3 At Christmas we decorate the house with .... balloons.
4 On Guy Fawkes' night in England, many people set off .... fireworks.
5 Having a party is the .... way to celebrate your birthday.
6 My mother always makes .... food on Christmas Day.
7 I always wear my .... clothes on the 4th of July.
8 In Britain, people believe that a rabbit's foot can bring .... luck.

8 Read the short texts and replace the adjectives in bold with adjectives from the lists.

exciting, smart, delicious, colourful

A At a birthday party children usually wear **1) nice** clothes and **2) bright** party hats. They eat **3) nice** food and they play some **4) good** games.

beautiful, formal, special

B The wedding day is a very **1) important** day for the couple. The bride wears a **2) nice** white wedding dress and the groom wears a **3) nice** suit.

difficult, magnificent, huge

C Carnival in my country is like a **1) big** street party. We stand at the side of the road and watch the dancers in their **2) great** costumes as they perform their **3) hard** dance routines.

21

Happy New Year!

STUDY TIP

When we describe a celebration we can start by telling the reader the name, place and time of the event as well as the reason people celebrate it.

9 Read the texts and fill in the names of the festivals: *Mothering Sunday, Hallowe'en, St Valentine's day*

A On February 14th, people in Britain and many other countries celebrate .... This is the day when we send special cards and gifts to the people we love.

B In Britain, ... takes place during the month of March. It is a special time when children and adults do special things for their mothers.

C In America, children celebrate .... on the 31st of October. It is a day when they wear costumes and go from house to house asking for sweets.

10 Use the notes and write a short introduction about the carnival in Rio.

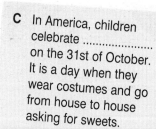

name: carnival
time: in the last few days before Lent
place: Rio de Janeiro, Brazil
reason: to eat, drink, dance and have fun before Lent begins

STUDY TIP

To describe a celebration we talk about what people do before the event and what they do during it.

11 The following sentences describe how the Brazilians celebrate carnival. Read the list of activities and fill in the table with the correct letters. Then say which take place <u>before</u> and which <u>during</u> carnival.

a bands play to crowds of excited people
b people make colourful costumes and masks
c people stand and watch the parades
d bands practise their music
e there is a big Samba competition
f dancers spend hours practising their dances
g dancers dance along the streets
h people throw confetti and dance

BEFORE	
DURING	*a*

Is there a similar celebration in your country? How do you celebrate it? Make a similar list, then talk about it.

12 Put the sentences into the correct order. What celebration is each sentence about?

1 cut / to make / people / flowers / garlands
People cut flowers to make garlands. (May Day)
2 buy / special lanterns / to make / pumpkins / people
3 flowers / buy / for / people / their loved ones
4 the tree / put / on / people / beautiful / decorations
5 play / on each other / tricks / people

STUDY TIP

Include people's feelings when you describe a celebration.

13 Read the sentences and underline the words which show how people feel.

It's a wonderful day. Everyone has fun and really enjoys themselves.

It's a very special day. Everyone feels proud and pleased with themselves.

It's a fantastic day. Everyone is excited and feels lucky to take part in the celebration.

STUDY TIP

A topic sentence is a sentence which says in brief what the paragraph is about.

14 Read the article and fill in the missing topic sentences.

a During the celebration the whole city changes.
b Everyone has fun.
c Preparations start months before.

Carnival in Rio
by Sally Scott

In my country, Brazil, we celebrate carnival at the end of February. It's a great time for everyone to have fun before the fasting period of Lent.

[1] People make colourful costumes and masks. The bands practise their music. There is a big Samba competition so the dancers spend hours practising their dances.

[2] The dancers dance along the streets. People stand and watch the parades. They throw confetti and dance along the streets.

[3] It's a very special celebration no one should miss because everyone has great fun.

Now answer the questions.

1 Which paragraph is about what people do before the celebration?
2 Which paragraph is about people's feelings?
3 Which paragraph is about what people do during the celebration?
4 Which paragraph is about the name/place/time/reason for the event?

WRITING

TIP

When you describe a celebration, you divide your description into four paragraphs. You start by saying what the event is (name), when and where it happens and what people celebrate (reason). Then you talk about what happens before and during the event. Remember to include adjectives *e.g. colourful, marvellous, delicious, etc.* You finish your description by saying how people feel.

15 The following sentences describe how people usually celebrate birthday parties. Read the list of activities and say which take place <u>before</u> and which <u>during</u> the party.

- wear paper hats
- hire a magician
- play games
- decorate the house
- give bags with little presents to guests
- make a birthday cake
- write invitations

- dance
- buy crisps and popcorn
- open presents
- blow out the candles on the cake

16 Use the information from Ex. 15 and the plan below to write an article about how people usually celebrate birthdays in your country. You can use your own ideas as well. Start like this: *Birthdays celebrate the day we were born. In my country we usually celebrate birthdays at home with a birthday party for friends.*

Plan

Paragraph 1: name, time, place, reason for the celebration
↓
Paragraph 2: activities before a birthday party
↓
Paragraph 3: activities during a birthday party
↓
Paragraph 4: people's feelings about a birthday party

For Sale!

A

B

1 First read the notices on the school notice-board below and match them to the pictures. Then read them again and answer the questions that follow.

1. To Bob Smith

I am interested in buying your bike. Please can you give me some information about it?
Jim Butler   Class 2B

3. WANTED

Large rucksack
Can pay up to £25
Call John Lee   Tel.: 6334140

2. FOR SALE

Mountain Bike
Good Condition
Bargain Price
Contact Bob Smith
Class 6D

4. FOR SALE

Two cute puppies
6 weeks old
Contact Sally Phillips
Class 5C

5. FOR SALE

Stereo system
Almost new
Great price
Contact Mary Green
Class 3A

C

1 Who wants to sell something? What is it?

2 Who wants to buy something? What is it?

3 Which notices give information about something which is for sale?

4 Which notice asks for information about something?

2 Read Bob's reply to Jim's note. Parts of the mountain bike are highlighted in the text. Find these parts in the picture and label them, as in the example.

D

3 ....

2 ....

4 ....

5 ....

1 *front light*

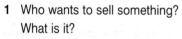

6 ....

Dear Jim,

Thanks for your note. Here is some information about the bike.

It is a large red mountain bike with black rubber **handlebars**. It's three years old and is in excellent condition. It's got ten **gears** and the **brakes** work very well. It has a **front light**, but it hasn't got a back light. It's got a comfortable, brand new leather **saddle**. The only problem is that it needs a new **back tyre**.

I'm selling it because I want to buy a motor bike. I would like £50 for it, but we can discuss the price.

I hope this tells you everything you need to know.

Bob Smith

3 Read Bob's letter again and answer the questions below.

1 Does Bob's letter ask for or give information?
2 What does Bob describe in his letter?
3 What colour is it?
4 How old is it?
5 What condition is it in?
6 How many gears has it got?
7 Has it got a front light?
8 The bike has got one new part. What is it?
9 What is the saddle made of?
10 Is there anything wrong with the bike?
11 Why is Bob selling his bike?
12 How much money does he want for it?

	OPINION	SIZE	AGE	COLOUR	MATERIAL/ TYPE	NOUN
It is a		large		red	mountain	bike.
It's got				black	rubber	handlebars.
It's got a	comfortable		new		leather	saddle.

5 Write the adjectives from the list below in the correct column.

old, thin, grey, plastic, young, blue, small, five-year-old, metal, short, paper, green, rubber, large, white, red, leather, long, brand new, glass, tiny, tall, brown, cotton, big, wooden

SIZE	AGE	COLOUR	MATERIAL/ TYPE
thin	*old*	*grey*	*plastic*
....	....	....	....
....	....	....	....
....	....	....	....
....	....	....	....
....	....	....	....
....	....	....	....

> **STUDY TIP**
>
> **Opinion adjectives** are those which express our personal opinion: that is, **what we think about something** (e.g. beautiful, ugly, comfortable, cute, etc). **Fact adjectives** are those which express facts: that is, **what something really is** (e.g. red, long, old, leather, etc).
>
> An *opinion* adjective goes before a *fact* adjective.
> e.g. It is a **beautiful red** mountain bike. (*beautiful* is an **opinion** adjective. - *red* is a **fact** adjective.)

4 Put the adjectives in the correct order, as in the example.

e.g. It's a ...*beautiful black*... vase.   (black/beautiful)

1 It's a .... chair. (leather/comfortable)
2 She's got a .... lamp. (green/pretty)
3 Look at this .... dress. (silk/lovely)
4 It's a(n) .... chair. (plastic/ugly)
5 Pam's got a .... kitten. (white/cute)
6 He's got a(n) .... house. (old/wonderful)

> **STUDY TIP**
>
> When you describe something you want to sell, you may use a **variety of adjectives** to describe it **in detail**. When you use two or more adjectives, you must always put them in the **correct order**. We don't normally use more than **two** or **three** adjectives to describe a noun.

6 Put the adjectives in brackets in the correct order, as in the example.

e.g. It's a ...*large leather*... (large, leather) bag.

1 It's a .... (cotton, brown, big) rucksack.
2 We've got a .... (black, young) puppy.
3 They are .... (long, green) trousers.
4 She's got a ....
(tiny, paper, yellow) hat.
5 I like this .... (old, wooden) bed.
6 He is selling his ....
(brand new, white) Porsche.

7 Look at the pictures below and describe them, as in the example. Use adjectives from Ex. 5.

e.g. *7 It's a pair of **long yellow rubber** flippers.*

1 radio 　2 mailbox 　3 boxing gloves

4 safety helmet

5 shirt 　6 briefcase

7 flippers 　8 golf shoes

8 Look at the above pictures again and the words below. Ask and answer questions, as in the example.

rubber, plastic, cotton, leather, wood, metal

e.g. ***What** are the flippers **made of**?*
*They are **made of rubber**.*

WRITING

TIP

When you write **notices,** you only need to write the **important words**. You do not need to write full sentences. You can **omit** some **articles, pronouns, verbs** and **prepositions. Notices should be short.** They do not include detailed descriptions.

9 Look at the notices below. Write them out in full sentences and underline the important words, as in the examples.

WANTED

Large suitcase
Can pay up to £20
Call Bill Sanders
Tel.: 6318437

e.g. *I'm interested in buying a **large suitcase.** I can pay up to **£20** for it. Please **call** me. My name is **Bill Sanders** and my **telephone number** is **6318437**.*

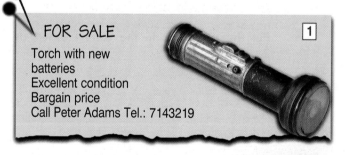

FOR SALE

Wooden chess board
2 years old
Contact Sarah Miles
Class 5A

e.g. *I'm selling a **wooden chess board**. It is **two years old**. Please **contact Sarah Miles** . I am in **Class 5A**.*

FOR SALE 　1

Torch with new batteries
Excellent condition
Bargain price
Call Peter Adams Tel.: 7143219

....
....
....

WANTED 　2

Two tickets for Sunday's football match
Front row seats
Can pay up to £50 each
Contact Steve Fonda Class 5C

....
....
....

FOR SALE `3`

Two adorable kittens
Brother and sister
Seven weeks old
Call Keith Ford
Tel.:7157707

....
....

WANTED `4`

Grey and white ski boots
Size: 40
Can pay up to £40
Call Chris Scott
Tel.: 6320001

....
....
....

10 Read the following short texts and underline the most important words. Then, write notices using the underlined words, as in the example below.

*e.g. I'm interested in buying **two tickets for The Rovers** **concert next Friday**. The **seats** must be **in or near the front row**. I can pay up to **£20** for **each ticket**. Please **call** me. My name is **Jan** and my **telephone number** is **7140019**.*

WANTED
e.g.
Two tickets for *The Rovers*
concert next Friday
Seats in or near front row
Can pay up to £20 each
Call Jan Tel.: 7140019

1 I'm selling a brass trumpet. It sounds great and it is in perfect condition. It's twelve years old and I am asking £60 for it. Please call me. My name is Stewart Green and my telephone number is 6335678.

....
....
....
....

2 I am interested in buying a waterproof watch. I need it for scuba-diving. I can only pay up to £30. Please contact Ed. I am in Class 3B.

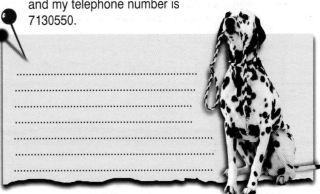
....
....
....
....
....
....

3 I'm selling a small collection of old teddy bears. They are all hand-made. They are in very good condition. I'm selling them at a great price. Please contact Sonia Miller in Class 4A.

....
....
....
....
....
....

4 I'm interested in buying a female Dalmatian. She must be at least one year old and house-trained. I can pay up to £200. Please call me. My name is Sandra Fox and my telephone number is 7130550.

....
....
....
....
....
....

11 PROJECT
Use the pictures from the *Photo File* section at the back of the book and write two notices for *something you want to buy* and two for *something you want to sell*. Write only the most important words in your notices.

It's a Bargain!

1 Read the advertisement and the two letters in Ex. 2, then answer the following questions.

    1 Which letter asks for information?
    2 Which letter gives information?
    3 How does each letter start and finish?
    4 Which letter includes a detailed description of the TV?
    5 Does the advertisement also include a detailed description of the TV?

2 Read the two letters again and correct the following statements. Then, in pairs, ask and answer questions about the two letters, as in the example below.
e.g. A: How big is the TV screen?
      B: The TV screen is twenty inches.

FOR SALE

Colour TV with remote control handset
Portable - Two years old
Fantastic price

Contact Mark Peters
Box 002

A

Dear Mark,

I am interested in buying your TV but I have some questions.
First of all, how big is the screen? You say it comes with a remote control handset, but has it got new batteries? You also say the TV is two years old, but is it in good condition? Can you tell me exactly how much you want for it and why you are selling it?
Please let me know when I can come and see it.

Thanks,
Jane Roberts

B

Dear Jane,

Thanks for your note. Here is some information about the TV.
First of all, the screen is twenty inches. It comes with a remote control handset with brand new batteries. The TV is black and grey. It's portable and it's got a plastic handle. It's in excellent condition, but I'm selling it because I want to buy a bigger one. I want £55 for it, but we can talk about that when you come to see it. I am at home from five o'clock every evening, so you can come and see the TV any time after that.
I hope this tells you everything you need to know.

Mark Peters

---

1 Mark is interested in buying the TV.
....
....

2 Jane is giving information about the TV.
....
....

3 The screen is sixteen inches.
....
....

4 The TV does not come with a remote control handset.
....
....

5 The TV is in poor condition.
....
....

6 It costs thirty-two pounds.
....
....

3 Look at the following beginnings and endings and say which are from:
a) *letters giving information about something.*
b) *letters asking for information about something.*

A Thanks for your note. Here is some information about the video cassette player I'm selling.

I hope this information helps you.

B I'm writing to give you some more information about the school play.

If you have any more questions, please call me on this number ...

C I want to know a few more things about the puppies you advertised in ...

Please call me at home. My number is 6120439.

D I'm interested in buying your microscope, but I've got a few questions.

Please let me know soon.

E I need to know more about the personal stereo you are selling.

Please can you give me the details soon?

F Here's the information you wanted about the tent.

Please let me know if you are still interested in buying it.

4 You are interested in buying the **TV set Mark Peters** is selling. Read the telephone conversation between you and Mark, and fill in the missing words.

Mark: Hello?
You: Hello, I'm **1)** .... I'm interested in buying your TV set. How **2)** .... it?
Mark: It's only two years old.
You: What **3)** .... it?
Mark: It's black and grey.
You: How **4)** .... screen?
Mark: It's twenty inches.
You: Is **5)** .... ?
Mark: Yes, it is, and it's got a plastic handle.
You: Does **6)** .... a remote control handset?

Mark: Yes, it does, and it's got brand new batteries.
You: Why **7)** .... it?
Mark: Because I want to buy a bigger one.
You: How **8)** .... for it?
Mark: I want £55 for it.
You: Oh, that sounds great! When can I come and see it?
Mark: Is tomorrow evening okay for you?
You: Yes, that's fine.

5 Work in pairs. Look at these two advertisements and act out dialogues asking for and giving information about the two items.

FOR SALE
Small hair-drier
Perfect for travelling
Good price - Needs plug
Call Emily White Tel.: 6380550

FOR SALE
Talking calculator
Needs new batteries
Cheap - only £5
Call Ross Milton Tel.: 8883400

STUDY TIP

Adjectives describe nouns. Adverbs describe verbs.
*e.g. The motorbike is in **good** condition. The motorbike runs **well**.*
*It's an **economical** car. It runs **economically**.*
(**Good** and **economical** are adjectives. **Well** and **economically** are adverbs.)

6 Fill in the sentences below with the correct adverb.

1 The camera isn't in **good** condition.
The camera doesn't work ....*well*........................
2 It's a very **slow** train.
The train moves very ....
3 My computer is **quick**.
My computer works ....
4 His old clock is in **wonderful** condition.
His old clock works ....
5 My new puppy is very **good**.
My new puppy behaves ....

It's a Bargain!

7 Read the following extracts from letters giving information and fill in the table.

A *They're a pair of black binoculars. They are fifteen years old but they work very well. They've got a brown leather strap but they need a new one. I'm selling them because I want to buy a new pair. I want £18 for them.*

B *The chair is blue with black plastic arms. It's only six months old and it's in great condition. There is nothing wrong with it. I want to sell it because I'm moving. The price is £20.*

C *My motorcycle is ten years old. It is red, blue and white with chrome handlebars. It's in perfect condition, but it needs one new mirror. I'm selling it because I need the money. The price is a real bargain. I only want £1,000 for it!*

	BINOCULARS	CHAIR	MOTORCYCLE
AGE?	15 years old		
COLOUR?		blue with black plastic arms	
CONDITION?			perfect
ANYTHING WRONG?			
WHY SELLING?			
HOW MUCH?			

Now use the information from the table above to ask and answer questions, as in the example.

e.g. A: How old are the binoculars?
B: They are fifteen years old.
A: What colour are they?
B: They are black with a ...

8 Put the words below in the correct order, as in the example.

e.g. brand / it's / red / a / new / bike
It's a brand new red bike.

1 it / very / works / well
....

2 for / I / want / it / £20
....

3 a / handle / new / it / needs
....

4 it's / bag / a / green / leather / with / handle / a / gold
....

5 needs / the / new / radio / batteries
....

6 it / selling / am / I / because / money / need / the / I
....

7 excellent / it's / condition / in
....

8 nothing / with / is / wrong / the / there / lamp
....

9 Read Sarah's letter giving information about a fan she's selling. Then, fill in the gaps using words from the list below.

everything, only, some, because, well, for, but, with, anything, also

Dear Jack,
   Thanks for your note. Here's 1) ...**some**... information about the fan.
   It's black 2) .... grey blades. It's 3) .... two years old. It has got three speeds and it works very 4) .... There isn't 5) .... wrong with it, 6) .... it needs a new plug. I'm selling it 7) .... I'm moving and I 8) .... need the money. I want £15 9) .... it.
   I hope this tells you 10) .... you need to know.

          Sarah Jones

10 Read the following description of a desk lamp. There are six mistakes in it. Find the mistakes and correct them.

It is a electric desk lamp. It has red and yellow with a blue plastic base. It need a plug and a new light bulb. There hasn't anything wrong with it and it works well. I am sell it because I have bought another one. I wanting £10 for it.

FOR SALE

Clock radio with alarm
5 years old - Great price
Contact Eve Dyllan
Box 343

- size?
- colour?
- handle?
- portable?
- take batteries?
- condition?

WRITING

TIP

When you write **a letter asking for information** about something you want to buy, ask detailed questions about its **age, size, colour, condition, price,** if anything is wrong with it, and why the person is selling it.

TIP

When you write a **letter giving information** about something you want to sell, make sure you **describe it in detail,** (age, size, colour, type of material, etc). Use **adjectives** in the correct order. **Adverbs** (well, perfectly, etc) can be included in your description, too.

11 Choose one of the advertisements and write two letters: one *asking for information* and the other *giving information* about what is for sale. Use the plans below and the information given next to each advertisement.

Plan A (asking for information)

Paragraph 1: reason for writing

Paragraph 2: detailed questions about what is for sale

Paragraph 3: closing remarks (Let me know when I can come and see it, etc)

Plan B (giving information)

Paragraph 1: reason for replying

Paragraph 2: detailed description of what is for sale / reason for selling it / price / when the person can see it

Paragraph 3: closing remarks (Hope this tells you everything, etc)

FOR SALE

Set of golf clubs with
blue bag
Three years old
Fantastic price
Contact Maria Lee
Box 517

FOR SALE

Exotic parrot
8 months old
Reasonable price
Contact Alex Walters
Box 303

- how many?
- for adults or children?
- leather bag?
- condition?
- how much?

- male/female?
- cage?
- talk?
- healthy?
- what/eat?
- how much?

Do's and Don'ts

1 Which picture shows?

1 a pedestrian crossing? ....
2 a path? ....
3 an accident? ....
4 a traffic sign? ....
5 a pavement? ....

B

2 Read the leaflet and answer the questions.

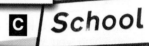
C **School**

The Rules of the Road

- Check your bicycle regularly. If you **check the lights, brakes and tyres**, you will be safer.

- Always **wear light-coloured clothes** at night. If you wear dark clothes, drivers can't see you.

- Always **wear a helmet** when you ride your bicycle. If you wear a helmet, you won't **hurt your head** in case of an accident.

- Never carry anything on the handlebars. If you have bags on the handlebars, you can't **ride your bicycle** properly.

- Make sure you **give a clear hand signal** when you want to turn left or right. If you signal, car drivers will know where you are going.

- Do not ride your bicycle on the pavement. If you ride on the pavement, you will cause problems for pedestrians.

D

E

1 What must you check on your bicycle? Why?

2 What kind of clothes must you wear at night? Why?

3 What must you wear on your head? Why?

4 Why mustn't you carry bags on the handlebars?

5 What must you do if you want to turn left or right? Why?

6 Where mustn't you ride your bicycle? Why?

3a Read the text of Ex. 2 again and label the pictures with the expressions in bold.

1 .... 2 ....

3 .... 4 ....

5 .... 6 ....

b Fill in: *wear a helmet, hurt your head, give a clear hand signal, wear light-coloured clothes, ride a bicycle, check the lights*

1 *...Check the lights...*, otherwise you won't be able to see when you ride at night.
2 Wear a helmet or you'll ....
3 .... so that drivers can see you at night.
4 Always .... when you want to turn.
5 Some people find it easy to learn to ....
6 Motorcyclists must always ....

4 Match the words to their meaning.

1 regularly
2 hurt
3 check
4 properly
5 signal
6 pedestrian

a make sure sth works/is okay
b sign
c often
d cause pain to sth/sb
e correctly
f sb walking near a road

We use **must** and **mustn't** to talk about rules or warnings.

Must means that someone is obliged to do something. *e.g. You **must** check the brakes.*

Mustn't means that someone isn't allowed to do something; it's against the rules. *e.g. You **mustn't** ride your bicycle on the pavement. (It isn't allowed)*

We use **imperative** or **no+noun/-ing form** for written notices describing warnings. *e.g. **Keep** door closed. Please **do not litter**.*
No entry. No smoking.

5 Look at the notices below and make dialogues using *must* or *mustn't*, as in the example. Where can you see such notices?

e.g. A: What does this sign mean?
B: It means you must keep the door closed.
A: Where can you see such a sign?
B: In a bank.

6 Match the signs to their meanings, then say what each sign means using *must* or *mustn't*.

a) stop, b) be careful of wild animals, c) be careful of school children, d) no parking, e) turn left, f) drive slowly, g) turn right, h) be careful of pedestrians, i) be careful of road workers

1 ....c.........   2 ....   3 ....

4 ....   5 ....   6 ....

7 ....   8 ....   9 ....

7 Rewrite the sentences in the form of written rules. Use *the imperative*, as well as *always, never* or *make sure*. Where would you read these rules?

1 You must sound the alarm if you smell smoke.
Sound the alarm if you smell smoke.
Always sound the alarm if you smell smoke.

2 You must find out where the emergency exits are.
....
....

3 You mustn't return to collect your belongings.
....
....

4 You mustn't leave cigarettes burning.
....

5 You mustn't run in the corridor.
....

6 You mustn't use the lift.
....

7 You must close doors behind you.
....

8 You mustn't leave bags or parcels on the stairs.
....
....

8 Match the hypotheses with the results then make sentences as in the example using *can, will, could may, might*.

e.g. If you wear a seatbelt, you will be safer in an accident.

HYPOTHESES

1 wear a seatbelt
2 brakes not work properly
3 give clear signals
4 look both ways before crossing the road
5 play in the road
6 not learn what the traffic signs mean

RESULTS

A car drivers know where you are going
B not pass your driving test
C be safer in an accident
D car hit you
E not be able to stop
F see any traffic that is coming

9 **Correct the mistakes. Which of these rules refer to a) pedestrians, b) motorcyclists or c) both?**

1 You always wear a helmet when you are riding a motorbike.
2 Don't never play in the road.
3 You make sure to learn what the traffic signs mean.
4 Not ride a motorbike if you are under 17.
5 To make sure you stop at traffic lights if they are red.
6 Always you look both ways carefully before you cross the road.

WRITING

TIP

When we write leaflets giving rules, regulations, instructions etc. we write each rule separately. We use the imperative as well as expressions such as **always, never, make sure**, etc.

We sometimes give a reason why we should do what the rule says. To do so, we use 1st type if -clauses.

e.g. Never carry more than one passenger. ***If you carry more passengers, the police may stop you.***

10 **Look at the pictures and the prompts. Then write a safety leaflet for pedestrians, as in the example. Give reasons.**

SAFETY RULES FOR PEDESTRIANS

e.g. Never play in the road. If you play in the road, a car may/might run you over.

- play / in the road - car run you over

- run / in / road- you fall and hurt yourself

- walk / the pavement - you not cause problems to car drivers

- cross / road / between / parked cars - you not see any traffic that is coming

- cross / road / at pedestrian crossing - you get across the road safely

11 **First match the hypotheses to the results, then say which picture matches each regulation. Finally, join the sentences using if.**

e.g. If you stop to help you may save someone's life.

HYPOTHESES	RESULTS
a stop to help	1 the injured can be taken to hospital
b move anybody in the car	2 may save someone's life
c call for an ambulance	3 can seriously injure the trapped person
d warn other drivers	4 keep them warm
e cover the injured with a blanket or coat	5 may prevent another accident

1 .... 2 .... 3 ....

4 .... 5 ....

12 **Use the pictures from the Photo File section to write a safety leaflet about what you must do if you see an accident. Use the *imperative* as well as expressions such as: *always, never* or *make sure*.**

35

Every Picture Tells a Story!

Who: *Jim*

Feelings:

Weather:

Time of day:

STORY A

1 The picture shows a scene from the beginning of a story. Look at it and fill in the balloons. Now, read the beginning of the story below and answer the questions.

Where:
Outside his house

"Please collect the mail!" Jim's mother shouted to him that cold, snowy morning. Outside, everything was still and white; even the birds were silent. Jim was whistling happily as he walked through the snow to the mailbox. Then he saw the package. It had his name on it in big red letters.

1 Who was involved in the story?
2 Where was he?
3 What time of day was it?
4 What was the weather like?
5 What did he do?
6 How do you think he felt?

- **Now read the beginning again and underline:**
  a the sentence which uses *direct speech*,
  b the adjectives which describe *the weather*,
  c the words which describe *the atmosphere*, and
  d the sentence which creates *mystery* or *suspense*.

- **How can you begin a story?**
- **Can you think of a title for the story?**

STORY C

3 Look at the picture and the notes for a story entitled *Alone in the Forest*. First tell the beginning of the story, then write it out, including information about the <u>place</u>, the <u>time</u>, and the <u>people</u> involved.

STORY B

2 Look at this picture and, using the notes below, tell the beginning of the story. Then, answer the questions and write out the beginning of the story.

- "Keep still, Barkley!"
- sunny morning/clear blue sky
- busy/noisy road
- Peter/carry/Barkley across the street
- suddenly/he/notice/man/with a camera

1 Who was involved in the story?
2 Where were they?
3 Was it morning or night?
4 What was the weather like?
5 How did Peter feel?
6 What do you think happened next?

- beautiful/sunny morning
- Danny/family/be/on camping holiday/ near/big forest
- Forest/seem/exciting/ magical
- Suddenly/he hear/strange noise
- Danny/decide/go/forest/ explore

36

4 The picture below shows a scene from the *ending* of **STORY A**. First, look at the picture and try to guess what happened at the end of this story. Then read the ending and answer the questions that follow.

Jim felt really glad and excited as he sat at his desk. His teacher was smiling at him as though she knew something. "Was it from you?" Jim asked. But she didn't answer. He still doesn't know who sent the package. There is one thing he is certain about though — that was the best birthday he ever had!

1 How did Jim feel at the end of the story?
2 What were Jim's exact words to his teacher?
3 What was the teacher's reaction?
4 What was the mystery in the story?

● **How** can you **end** a story?

5 Look at the picture and guess what happened at the end of **STORY B**. Now use the following notes to answer the questions. Finally, first tell, then write the ending of the story about Barkley.

● Peter/feel/proud/of Barkley
● the film/be/big hit
● "Well done, Superdog!"
● that morning/he receive/letter
● guess who/want Barkley/next film?

1 How did Peter feel about Barkley?
2 What was a success?
3 What did Peter say to him?
4 What did Peter receive that morning?
5 Was he surprised? Why?

6 Look at the picture and the notes below then tell the ending of the story, *Alone in the Forest.*

● Danny/feel/relieved
● he/be/safe again/his family
● the forest/be/dark, mysterious place
● Danny/be/very lucky/to be/home again
● he/still/remember/his father's words
● "Don't ever go into the forest alone!"

7 Replace the words in bold with appropriate ones with a similar meaning from the list.

silent, mail, certain, collect, package, still

1 Mr Johnson asked his son to **fetch** his suit from the cleaners.
2 Pam sat quietly at her desk and opened her **letters**.
3 There was no wind at all and the lake was very **calm**.
4 When all the guests left, the room became **quiet**.
5 Kim got a big **parcel** from her aunt in Australia.
6 The children were **sure** that he was the criminal.

8 Look at the beginning and ending of **STORY A** again. Find all the verbs in the past simple and underline them. Then, write them in the correct list. Write the verbs only once.

Regular verbs: shouted, ...
....
Irregular verbs: was, ...
....

9 In turns, use the verbs from Ex. 8 to make sentences of your own, as in the examples.

e.g. *S1: Laura **shouted** for help but nobody could hear her.*
      *S2: There **was** a strange old hotel in the distance.*

Every Picture Tells a Story!

STUDY TIP

- We use the **past simple** and the **past continuous** in stories **to set the scene**.
  e.g. Jim **was whistling** happily as he **walked** through the snow.

10 Put the verbs in brackets into the *past simple* or *past continuous*.

Edwin 1) .... (look) at the high stone wall. The sky was grey and it 2) .... (rain). Suddenly, he 3) .... (hear) a dog barking. Edwin 4) .... (want) to climb over the wall but he 5) .... (be) afraid of the dog. It 6) .... (not /sound) friendly. He 7) .... (take) a deep breath and 8) .... (begin) to climb. He 9) .... (know) Sally 10) .... (be) on the other side of the wall. She 11) .... (wait) desperately for his help. "I'm coming!" he 12) .... (shout).

STUDY TIP

We can form **adjectives from some nouns by** adding **-y**.
e.g. snow - snow**y**
Jim's mother shouted to him that cold **snowy** morning.
(**Snowy** is an adjective which describes the weather.)

11 Complete the table, as in the examples.

Noun	Adjective	Noun	Adjective
1 wind	*windy*	6 storm	....
2 *sun*	sunny	7	foggy
3	cloudy	8 ice	....
4	rainy	9	misty
5 snow	....	10 chill	....

Now, choose adjectives from the table above to make your own sentences, as in the example.

e.g. *The sky grew dark and* **cloudy** *and soon it began to rain.*

38

12 Look at the adjectives in the list and match them to the pictures.

happy, worried, angry, scared, confused, tired

1 Liz - ....
2 Tom - ....
3 Ann - ....
4 Bob - ....
5 Sue - ....
6 Steve - ....

Now use the adjectives to make sentences, as in the example.

e.g. **Liz** *felt* **angry** *when her son made such a silly mistake.*

13 First explain the adjectives in the list below, then use them to make the sentences more interesting, as in the example. You can use the adjectives more than once.

brown, old, beautiful, cool, wooden, strange, big, calm, burning, grey, hot, dangerous

1 Barbara screamed when she saw the bear.
  e.g. *Barbara screamed when she saw the* **big brown** *bear.*
2 Alex touched the door with his hand.
3 Ed went swimming in the lake.
4 John walked through the forest.
5 He was afraid of the wolves.
6 Jim sat next to the fire.
7 Christine watched the man getting into the car.
8 Danny saw a package.

UNIT 9

WRITING

14 Look at the pictures and the words below and try to guess how this story *begins* and *ends*.

Never give up! After all, tomorrow is another day.

Now read the *beginning* and the *ending* of the story and underline:
a) the sentences which use *direct speech*,
b) the words which describe *the weather*,
c) the words which describe *the atmosphere*,
d) the words which describe *feelings*, and
e) the sentence which creates *mystery* or *suspense*.

BEGINNING
One sunny dry April morning, Martha was planting some seeds in her garden. The garden looked so peaceful and beautiful, but Martha was feeling really sad. She knew she could lose everything. "Oh no! What am I going to do?" she cried.

ENDING
When Martha got first prize for the best and biggest pumpkin, she felt happy, proud and relieved. Now she had the money to keep her farm. She remembered her grandmother's wise words: "Never give up! After all, tomorrow is another day."

TIP BEGINNING

You **begin a story** by **setting the scene**. Imagine that you are looking at a picture and describe the **place** (where), the **time** (when), the **weather**, the **people involved** (who) and their **feelings**. You can use someone's exact words **(direct speech)** to make your beginning more interesting.

TIP ENDING

You can **end a story** by describing people's **feelings** or **reactions**. You can use someone's exact words **(direct speech)** to make your ending more interesting. You can also **end a story** by creating **mystery** or **suspense**.

15 First *say* then *write* an interesting *beginning* and *ending* for the pictures below. Use the notes to help you.

- cold/misty/winter night
- Christine/sit/next to/ fireplace
- knit/scarf/for little boy/ Peter
- suddenly/strange/ noise/break/ peaceful silence/the night
- ..../call out

Who's there?

I'll be back! That's a promise!

- Christine/Peter/stand/outside/ the house
- they/feel/exhausted/but/glad/ because/ their nightmare/be/over
- as/they/watch/the/dangerous man/ get into/police car/he/turn around
- he/look at/them/with/cold/ black eyes
- he/threaten/them

39

A Summer's Tale!

1 The pictures tell a story. Look at them and point to the following things: *flippers, mask, knife, seal, net, rock, beach, fishing boat*. Now, answer the questions below.

1 Who was involved in the story?
2 Where was the girl?
3 What was the weather like?
4 How did the girl feel?
5 Why did the girl get into the water?

6 What did she see in the water?
7 What did she do then?
8 What happened at the end of the story?

2 Read the story below and write the topic of each paragraph in the bubbles provided.

- description of events before the main event
- setting the scene (who-where-when-what)

- ending (feelings and reactions)
- description of the main event

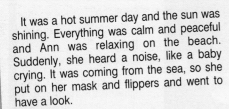

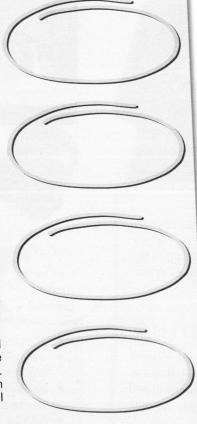

It was a hot summer day and the sun was shining. Everything was calm and peaceful and Ann was relaxing on the beach. Suddenly, she heard a noise, like a baby crying. It was coming from the sea, so she put on her mask and flippers and went to have a look.

As soon as she got into the water, she swam towards where the sound was coming from. After she had swum a short distance, she saw a fishing net. Then she saw the seal. It was crying because it had got caught in the net. Ann tried to help it, but she needed a knife.

Just then she heard the engine of a boat. She climbed onto a rock and saw a small fishing boat. She needed help quickly, so she started to wave. When the man in the boat saw Ann, he came immediately to help her. He had a knife, so together they cut a hole in the net. Two minutes later, the seal was free.

Before the seal swam away, Ann played with it for a while. They swam together in the calm blue sea and Ann felt really happy. Finally, when the seal decided to leave, Ann shouted to her new friend, "Good luck! I hope I'll see you again soon!"

STUDY TIP

When you write stories, use adjectives to describe the **weather** and **atmosphere**.
e.g. *It was a **hot**, summer day. (weather)*
*Everything was **calm** and **peaceful**. (atmosphere)*

3 Decide which of the adjectives below describe *weather* and which describe *atmosphere* and complete the tables.

strange, wet, cloudy, magical, sunny, windy, still, silent, foggy, noisy, calm, rainy

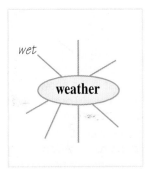

wet

weather

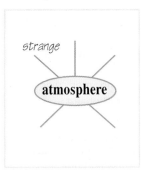

strange

atmosphere

Now use the adjectives to make up sentences of your own, as in the example.

e.g. *It was snowing and everything outside was **silent**.*

STUDY TIP

We use the **past simple** to talk about actions which happened at a specific time in the past. We use the **past continuous** to talk about an action which was happening at a specific time in the past.
e.g. *It was a hot summer day and the sun **was shining**.*
*Suddenly, she **heard** a noise.*

4 Put the verbs in brackets into the past simple or the past continuous.

1 It .... (**rain**) heavily and Pete .... (**drive**) very fast when he .... (**have**) an accident.
2 It .... (**snow**) heavily and the children .... (**make**) a snowman outside. Suddenly, a bright light .... (**appear**) in the sky.
3 One day, while I .... (**sit**) in the garden, I .... (**hear**) a strange noise. It .... (**come**) from the apple tree, so I .... (**go**) to have a look.
4 The sun .... (**shine**) and the birds .... (**sing**) so we .... (**decide**) to go for a picnic.
5 The wind .... (**blow**) through the trees and the wolves .... (**howl**) outside. Sandra .... (**feel**) really scared!

STUDY TIP

We use the **past perfect** to describe an action which happened before another action in the past.
e.g. *After she **had swum** a short distance, she saw a fishing net.*

5 Put the verbs in brackets into the correct tense: present perfect or past simple.

1 He ...*phoned*... (**phone**) the garage because his car ...*had broken down*... (**break down**).
2 She .... (**wash**) the dishes after she .... (**finish**) her meal.
3 Paul .... (**go**) to the doctor because he .... (**hurt**) his leg.
4 As soon as they .... (**do**) their homework, they .... (**go**) out to play.
5 The train .... (**leave**) two minutes before Pam .... (**arrive**) at the station.
6 I .... (**get**) wet because I .... (**forget**) to take my umbrella.

6 Read the short texts below and put the verbs in brackets into the past simple, past continuous or past perfect.

A The Ross family **1)** .... (**sit**) in the kitchen and Mrs Ross **2)** .... (**cook**) breakfast when her son **3)** .... (**walk**) through the door. It **4)** .... (**be**) his birthday and she **5)** .... (**promise**) to buy him a new bike. After he **6)** .... (**eat**) his breakfast, she **7)** .... (**tell**) him to go outside to the garage.

B The band **1)** .... (**play**) her favourite song and everyone **2)** .... (**dance**). Alison's husband **3)** .... (**order**) some champagne. They **4)** .... (**start**) drinking it slowly. Then she **5)** .... (**notice**) that he **6)** .... (**hold**) a small silver box in his hand.

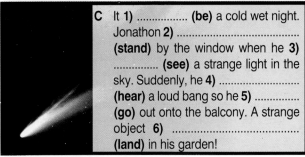

C It **1)** .... (**be**) a cold wet night. Jonathon **2)** .... (**stand**) by the window when he **3)** .... (**see**) a strange light in the sky. Suddenly, he **4)** .... (**hear**) a loud bang so he **5)** .... (**go**) out onto the balcony. A strange object **6)** .... (**land**) in his garden!

A Summer's Tale!

STUDY TIP

We use **time words** (first, as soon as, after, then, etc.) in stories to **make the order in which events happen clear to the reader**.

e.g. **As soon as** she got into the water, she swam ...
After she had swum a short distance, she ...
Then she saw the seal.

7 First read the story below and put the paragraphs in the correct order. Then, circle the correct time words.

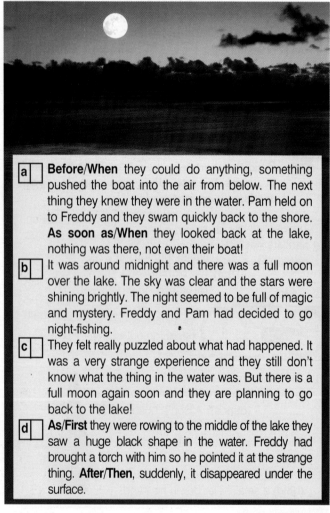

a **Before/When** they could do anything, something pushed the boat into the air from below. The next thing they knew they were in the water. Pam held on to Freddy and they swam quickly back to the shore. **As soon as/When** they looked back at the lake, nothing was there, not even their boat!

b It was around midnight and there was a full moon over the lake. The sky was clear and the stars were shining brightly. The night seemed to be full of magic and mystery. Freddy and Pam had decided to go night-fishing.

c They felt really puzzled about what had happened. It was a very strange experience and they still don't know what the thing in the water was. But there is a full moon again soon and they are planning to go back to the lake!

d **As/First** they were rowing to the middle of the lake they saw a huge black shape in the water. Freddy had brought a torch with him so he pointed it at the strange thing. **After/Then**, suddenly, it disappeared under the surface.

8 Read the story in Ex. 7 again and underline :

a) the sentence which describes *the weather.*
b) the sentence which describes *the atmosphere.*
c) the adjectives which describe *feelings.*
d) the sentence(s) which create(s) *mystery* or *suspense.*

Study these examples.

> *It was a hot summer day* **and** *the sun was shining.*
> *The seal was crying* **because** *it had got caught in the net.*
> *Then Ann saw a small fishing boat,* **so** *she climbed onto a rock.*

9 Join the two columns below to make complete sentences.

1 He opened the door	a **because** he was going to a party.
2 Suddenly, there was a knock on the door	b **and** it was snowing heavily.
3 It was New Year's Eve	c **and** saw an old man standing there.
4 The man was a millionaire	d **because** he had got lost in the snow.
5 The old man needed help	e **so** Tom went downstairs and opened it.
6 Tom was upstairs getting ready	f **so** he gave Tom a large reward for helping him.

Now put the sentences in the correct order and try to tell the story.

☐ ☐ ☐ ☐ ☐ ☐

10 CAN YOU WRITE A GOOD STORY?
Test yourself by answering these questions.

1 Which tense do we use to give background information?
   A past simple   B past continuous   C past perfect

2 Which paragraphs make up the main body of a story?
   A 1 and 2   B 3 and 4   C 2 and 3

3 Which paragraph describes the main event?
   A the third   B the second   C the first

4 Which paragraph sets the scene?
   A the second   B the third   C the first

5 Which tense do we use to describe an action which happened before another action in the past?
   A past perfect   B past simple   C past continuous

6 We never end a story by ...
   A writing "THE END" at the bottom of the page.
   B creating mystery or suspense.
   C using direct speech.

WRITING

> **TIP**
>
> When you write **a story**, divide it into **four paragraphs**. **Begin** your story **by setting the scene** (who, where, when, what, etc). In the **second paragraph**, describe the events which happened **before** the main event. In the **third paragraph**, describe the main event. **End** your story by describing people's **feelings** or **reactions**.
> You can use **direct speech** and a variety of **adjectives** to make your story more interesting to the reader. In stories we normally use **past tenses**. We also use **time words** (first, then, after, etc) to narrate the events in the order in which they happened.

11   Match the sentences to the pictures below.

1   Jennifer ran to the first door, rang the bell and shouted.
2   It was a cold, dark evening and the streets were empty.
3   "Don't worry! You left your handbag on the train!" the man explained.
4   Then, she heard footsteps behind her.

> Leave me alone! What do you want?

D ☐

A ☐

B ☐

> Help!

C ☐

First, answer the following questions, then tell the story by looking at the pictures.

1   What was the weather like?
2   Who was involved in the story?
3   Where and when did the story take place?
4   What did she see when she looked over her shoulder?
5   How do you think she felt?
6   What did she feel on her arm?
7   What did the man say?
8   What do you think happened at the end of the story?

12   Use the information from Ex. 11 and the plan below to write a story entitled *A Stranger in the Night*.

Plan

Paragraph 1:   set the scene (who, where, when, what)
↓
Paragraph 2:   describe the events which happened before the main event
↓
Paragraph 3:   describe the main event
↓
Paragraph 4:   end the story (refer to people's feelings and reactions/use direct speech)

Come to my Party!

1 Look at the picture and the invitation below and answer the questions.

To **Katie**

Debbie invites you to **her birthday** party at 7, Kings Road, Langley on **Saturday, 17th June** at **6 pm**.

1 Who is the invitation from?
2 Who is the invitation to?
3 What kind of party is it?
4 When is the party?
5 Where is the party?

2 Read Debbie's letter below and underline the correct word(s) in the sentences that follow.

7, Kings Road
Langley
Sussex
10th June, 19....

Dear Katie,

I'm writing to invite you to my birthday party on Saturday, 17th June. I hope you will be able to come. It will be really good to see you again.

Our new house has got a big garden so this year I'm going to have a barbecue. I'm sure it will be lots of fun. We're going to cook hamburgers and sausages and my mother's going to make a big salad. After the barbecue we're going to sing some songs around the fire. I expect Dad will sing some of his old songs too! I'm sure everyone will have a good time and I hope you will be able to join us.

I suppose you will come by train, so here are the directions from the station. When you come out of the station, turn left into Wayne Avenue. Walk to the end of the road and turn right into Green Road. Walk past the supermarket and the cinema. Go straight on until you see a baker's. The baker's is on your right, and our house is opposite on the left. It's got a blue door — you can't miss it!

The party is going to start at six o'clock. Faye and Alison are going to stay the night but there will be lots of room for you if you want to stay, too. Please come — we'll all have a great time. I'll see you on Saturday!

Lots of love,
Debbie

1 Debbie is going to have a **fancy dress party/birthday party**.
2 She is going to have a **barbecue/picnic** in her garden.
3 Her **dad/mum** is going to make a big salad.
4 Katie will probably go to Debbie's house by **bus/train**.
5 Debbie's house is opposite the **baker's/ cinema**.
6 The party is going to **start/finish** at six o'clock.

3 Read the letter again and decide which paragraph describes each of the topics below.

(details about the party (food, activities, etc)) — Paragraph ....2.....

(closing remarks) — Paragraph ....4.....

(reason for writing) — Paragraph ......1......

(directions to the house) — Paragraph .....3......

4 Look at the map. Draw a line from the station to Debbie's house by reading the directions in her letter.

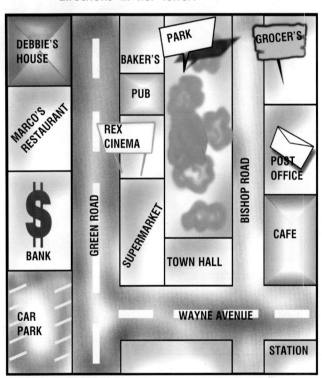

5 Debbie is giving another friend, Sam, directions to her house. Fill in the gaps with words from the list.

go past, next to, come out, go straight on, turn left

Sam: Hello, Debbie. I'm in the car park. Can you tell me how to get to your house from here?

Debbie: **1)** *Come out* of the car park on Green Road and **2)** .... **3)** .... until you see Marco's, an Italian restaurant. **4)** .... the restaurant and my house is right **5)** .... it. You can't miss it!

Sam: Thanks a lot! I'm on my way.

6 Now, in pairs, act out similar dialogues, as in Ex. 5. Take it in turns to be Debbie. Give directions to someone who is:

- at the bank
- at the Town Hall
- at the café
- at the post office

7 Read the following extract from a letter and fill in the gaps with words from the list.

out, opposite, across, by, to, on, off

You can come **1)** *by* bus from Langley. Get **2)** .... the bus at Victoria Station. Come **3)** .... of the station and turn right into Park Road. Walk **4)** .... the end of the road and turn left into Marble Street. Go straight **5)** .... until you get to the bridge. Then walk **6)** .... the bridge and you'll see a Post Office. My house is **7)** .... the Post Office. It's № 14.

┌─────────────────────────────────
STUDY TIP

- We **never use will after time expressions** such as: when, until, before, as soon as, etc.

e.g. **When** you ~~will~~ come out of the station, turn left. Go straight on **until** you ~~will~~ see a church.

8 Put the verbs in brackets into the present simple or the future simple.

1 I *will call* **(call)** you as soon as I *get* **(get)** to Susie's house.
2 We .... **(eat)** when everyone .... **(arrive)**.
3 Mum .... **(give)** Tony his present before he .... **(blow out)** the candles.
4 They .... **(serve)** drinks until the bar .... **(close)** at 11 p.m.
5 Walk straight on until you .... **(pass)** the supermarket.
6 When .... **(you/send)** the invitations for the party?
7 As soon as Kim .... **(arrive)**, we .... **(serve)** the meal.
8 When you .... **(get)** off the train, you .... **(see)** Jonathan on the platform.

STUDY TIP

- We use **going to** to express our **future plans** or **arrangements**.
- We use **will** to express **on-the-spot decisions**. We can also use **will** with the words: *think, hope, believe, probably, certainly*, etc.

e.g. I*'m going to* have a barbecue.
I hope you **will** be able to come.

9 Read Debbie's letter again and say what she is *going to* do and what she *hopes* or *thinks* will happen, as in the example.

e.g. Debbie **hopes** that Katie **will** be able to go to her party.
She is **going to** have a barbecue in the garden, etc.

10 Read the following dialogue and fill in the gaps with *will* or *be going to*, as in the example.

Joe: Hi, Tina. I **1)** *am going to* have a party for Sam on Saturday. He **2)** .... study in England, so it's a *Goodbye* party.

Tina: That sounds nice!

Joe: It's a surprise party, though. I **3)** .... tell Sam to come to my house at 8 o'clock. I don't think he **4)** .... guess that it's a party.

Tina: I **5)** .... probably come at 7 o'clock, so I **6)** .... be able to help you get things ready.

Joe: Oh, good! Laura **7)** .... bake a big cake and I **8)** .... order some pizzas and drinks from the Italian restaurant, around the corner.

Tina: I'm sure Sam **9)** .... love that. Pizza is his favourite food. I think he **10)** .... be really pleased!

Joe: Liz **11)** .... bring some of her CD's. I hope she **12)** .... bring some dance music, too.

Tina: I can't wait. I think everyone **13)** .... have a great time! I **14)** .... see you on Saturday, then.

11 Label the pictures with words from the list. Then tick which foods or drinks can be found at a barbecue.

pasta, sausages, hot dog, tea, steak, hamburger, milkshake, orange juice, soup, salad, prawns, chicken, pizza

1 ☐   2 ☐   3 ☐

4 ☐   5 ☐   6 ☐

7 ☐   8 ☐   9 ☐

10 ☐

11 ☐   12 ☐   13 ☐

12 Use words from Ex. 11 to make up dialogues, as in the example. Use *be going to* and *will*.

SA: Are you **going to** bring anything to the barbecue?
SB: I think I **will** bring some **steak**. What about you?
SA: I am **going to** bring some **salad**. I hope everyone **will like** it!, etc.

13 Read the letter of invitation to Tracy and underline the correct word. Then answer the following questions.

1 Who is the letter to? Who is it from?
2 Which paragraph mentions the reason for writing?
3 Which paragraph gives details about the party?
4 Which paragraph includes directions?
5 How does the writer close the letter?

Dear Tracy,

I hope you are 1) **good/well**. I'm writing to invite you 2) **to/at** a fancy dress party at my house. It's 3) **on/for** Sunday, 22nd March at seven o'clock.

I'm going to dress up 4) **with/as** *Zena, the Warrior* and my brother is going to come as *Hercules*. I think it will be really good fun! I hope you will 5) **can/be able to** come. My parents are going to 6) **order/ask** some take-away food from *Burger Land* in town. They are also going to give prizes for the 7) **best/better** costumes, so I'm sure everyone will have a great time.

You will probably come 8) **with/by** train, so here are the directions. When you 9) **come/will come** out of the station, turn left and walk to the end of Cherry Road. My house is the big white one 10) **in/on** your right next to the cinema.

I suppose the party will finish quite 11) **late/lately**, but you can stay the night at my house if you want to. It will be lovely to see you 12) **soon/again**.

Lots of love,
Susan

14 Match the following types of parties to the activities below.

1 Fancy dress party

2 Welcome Home party

3 Christmas party

4 *Farewell* party

5 Birthday party

a	We sing carols around the tree.
b	We blow out the candles on the cake and make a wish.
c	We give prizes for the best costumes.
d	We hang a *Welcome* sign outside the door.
e	We give souvenirs as leaving presents.

15 You are going to have a party. First decide on the type of the party, and then fill in the invitation card to your friend.

To ....
.... invites you to a ....
party at .... on
.... at .... pm.

WRITING

TIP

When you write a **letter to invite a friend to a party**, divide your letter into four paragraphs. **Start** your letter by stating the **reason for writing**. In the **second paragraph** give **details** about the party (type of party, people coming, food, etc). In the **third paragraph** give **directions** explaining how your friend can get to your house. **Close** your letter by saying you hope he or she will be able to come.

16 Use the plan below and the map from the Photo File section to write *a letter of invitation* to your friend for your party.

Plan

Dear *(your friend's first name)* ....,

Paragraph 1:
• reason for writing
• when/where the party is

Paragraph 2: details about the party (type, people coming, food, clothes, etc.)

Paragraph 3: directions to your house

Paragraph 4: closing remarks (I hope you will be able to come, etc)

Yours,

(your first name)
....

It Happened to me ...

1 Look at the Reader's Page and the picture and answer the questions.

1 Where can you see a big wheel like the one in the picture?
2 Who wrote the story?
3 Where did the story take place, at a fairground or at a circus?
4 Why do you think the ride took two hours?
5 What do you think the story is about?

BIG WHEEL
£1 FOR
A TWO-MINUTE RIDE!

Reader's Page
. . . .

It Happened to me ...

This week's story comes from fourteen-year-old Karen Morgan of Blackpool, England.

"They said the ride took two minutes — but it took two hours!"

2 Read Karen's story and answer the questions. Then read it again and underline the adjectives which describe Karen's and Sarah's feelings.

It happened one weekend while I was at the fairground. I was with my friend Sarah and we were both really excited. The flashing lights and bright colours made everything appear magical. We were having a great time and we had been on most of the rides when Sarah pointed to the big wheel. The sign said "£1 for a two-minute ride!"

At first I wasn't sure, but Sarah had been on it before. "It only takes two minutes," she said. "Come on — it's a really thrilling ride!" A minute later we were in the air. It was like flying! "This is amazing!" I shouted happily to Sarah.

Then, suddenly, there was a loud crash and everything stopped. I was really frightened! Sarah held my hand tightly because she was worried, too. We looked down and saw two mechanics. "Don't worry," they shouted. "It won't take us long to fix it!" So we waited ... and waited! At first we were amused. Everyone was running around below us. After a while though, it became scary up there.

Two hours later, the wheel finally started to move again. I was so happy. It had been a long, tiring evening. That two-minute ride had turned into a two-hour nightmare!

1 When and where did Karen's story take place?
2 Who was Karen with?
3 How did the two girls feel?
4 Did Karen want to go on the big wheel at first?
5 Did she finally decide to go on it?
6 What was it like?
7 What happened then?
8 Who came to fix the big wheel?
9 How did the two girls feel while they were waiting?
10 What happened at the end of the story? How did Karen feel?

48

3 What do these words mean? Look at the story in Ex. 2 and choose the correct meaning.

1 *fairground* means ...
  a car park
  (b) amusement park

2 *flashing* means ...
  a going on and off
  b going up and down

3 *thrilling* means ...
  a interesting
  b exciting

4 *tightly* means ...
  a firmly
  b quickly

5 *mechanic* means ...
  a person who sells machines
  b person who repairs machines

6 *fix* means ...
  a mend
  b break

4 Underline the correct adjective.

1 The children's visit to Disneyland was a **boring**/**magical** time for them.
2 We looked up at the **bright**/**tight** stars in the sky.
3 Ann and Bob were watching TV and were laughing at the comedian's **boring**/**amusing** story.
4 We all had a **great**/**long** time at the zoo yesterday. We really enjoyed it!
5 John decided to go to bed early last night because he had had a very **thrilling**/**tiring** day.
6 The dolphin at Sea World performed some **amazing**/**excited** tricks.

STUDY TIP

• Adjectives ending in **-ed** describe **how somebody feels**. *e.g. We were both really **excited**!*
• Adjectives ending in **-ing** describe **what somebody or something is like**. *e.g. It was a really **exciting** ride!*

5 Use the verbs in brackets to form adjectives, as in the example.

1 **(bore)** a. The film on TV was really *boring*, so I decided to go to the cinema.
       b. The children were *bored* during the Maths lesson.

2 **(thrill)** a. Going to see the Pyramids was a .... experience.
        b. Susan was .... with all her birthday presents.

3 **(fright)** a. The children were .... when they saw the monster and started to cry.
       b. When the lion escaped from its cage, it was a very .... moment.

4 **(amaze)** a. We had an .... view of the mountains from our hotel room.
        b. Julie was .... when she met the famous opera singer.

5 **(worry)** a. When the police came, Fiona had a very .... look on her face.
        b. It was a .... time for Mrs Barker when her son didn't come home from school.

6 **(tire)** a. Travelling from France to Spain by car was an extremely .... journey.
      b. David had had a very busy day and when he got home he was really ....

6 Read the extract below and correct the underlined mistakes, as in the example.

When we <u>arrived at home</u> very late last night, we realised that someone <u>broke</u> into our house. While <u>mine</u> husband <u>was called</u> the police, I looked around the house to see <u>who</u> was missing. The thieves had <u>steal</u> our new CD player <u>and</u> all the other electrical equipment was still there. Half an hour <u>after</u>, the police <u>arrive</u>. They asked us a lot of questions and wrote <u>anything</u> down. Then, suddenly, as they <u>was</u> leaving the telephone <u>rung</u>. "Hello? Who is it?" I asked <u>nervous</u>.

a *arrived home*
b ....
c ....
d ....
e ....
f ....
g ....
h ....
i ....
j ....
k ....
l ....
m ....

7 Fill in the gaps with the correct time word(s) from the list below.

before, until, just then, as soon as, finally, while, at first, later

On a cold dark January night, **1)** .... I was walking home through Fenn's Forest, I had a frightening experience. I had stayed at my friend's house **2)** .... late that night, so I was hurrying home. Suddenly, I heard a loud crash of thunder and it started raining heavily.

3) .... I panicked because I couldn't see my way clearly. I felt miserable and scared. **4)** .... a flash of lightning lit up the sky and I saw an old building ahead of me. I walked towards it and I realised that it was a rather strange little hotel.

Half an hour **5)** .... I was in bed in one of the hotel rooms. I had decided to spend the night there because of the storm. **6)** .... I had got into bed I heard an unusual frightening cry. I got up and saw a large black shape moving outside my window. I screamed in fear because I thought it was a ghost! I quickly ran downstairs to ask for help.

"Don't worry!" the hotel owner explained. "I should have told you **7)** .... you went up to your room. There's a noisy old owl which lives outside on the balcony." I went back to my room feeling a bit silly but extremely relieved at the same time. **8)** .... I was able to relax. It had been a long night!

Now, read the story again and look at the writer's notes below for the plot line of the first paragraph of the story. Complete his notes to make the plot line of the second, third and fourth paragraphs.

* *forest, cold, dark night, walking home, began to rain*

* ....
* ....
  ....
* ....
  ....
* ....
  ....

* When you write a story, you must write the events in **chronological order** using appropriate time words.
  e.g. Last weekend **while** I was at ...
  We were having a great time and we ...
  A minute later we were in the air.
  Then, suddenly, there was a loud crash and ...

8 The following events are from a story. Read them and put them into the correct chronological order.

a As soon as I got off the train, I ran up the steps and got a taxi back to the hotel. ☐

b Suddenly, there was a loud bang and a second later the train stopped. ☐

c I had an unusual train journey when I was on holiday in Moscow last year. ☐

d Twenty minutes later, the train slowly began to move again and everyone cheered. ☐

e It was my first day there, so I decided to go into the centre and do some shopping. ☐

f It was snowing heavily when I arrived at the Metro station, but I went in and soon my train came and I got on. ☐

WRITING

When you write **a story, first decide on the plot line** (what events you are going to include and in which order you are going to write them). Write an **interesting beginning** by setting the scene, **then** describe the events in the **main body** in the order they happened. **Finally** give your story **a good ending**. A **variety of adjectives** and the use of **direct speech** can make your story more interesting to the reader.

9 Imagine that the following pictures tell the story of something which happened to you last summer. Look at them and make notes for a plot line for each picture.

A

D

B

10 Look at the pictures in Ex. 9 again and match them with the following plot line notes. Then, using the notes, tell the class your story.

- *red truck appeared, men with fish came to help* ☐
- *relieved, thanked men, free tickets for circus* ☐
- *summer afternoon, arrived home after doing my shopping, saw bear in garden* ☐
- *shocked, climbed apple tree, bear followed* ☐

11 Use the pictures in Ex. 9, the information in Ex. 10 and the plan below to write your story for a short story competition in a magazine. The title for your story is: *It Happened to me ...*

C

Plan

Paragraph 1: set the scene (where, when, who, what)

Paragraphs 2, 3: describe the events before the main event and the main event itself

Paragraph 4: end the story (refer to people's feelings and reactions/use direct speech)

UNIT 13 UNIT

Who's Who?

1   2   3

1   Read the introduction to this magazine article and match the people in the pictures to the descriptions.

AWAY FROM HOME!

Mary Harris spoke to three people who are living in a foreign country. These three people are living in Britain. She asked them about their lives, their problems and their future plans.

A   Pablo is from Spain. He's studying Computer Science at London University.

B   Eva is from Poland. She's working in a factory and learning English.

C   Marco is from Italy. He's working as a chef at the Glitz Hotel.

2   Answer the following questions about Pablo, Eva and Marco.

1   What problems do you think these people have living away from home?
2   What do you think they like or dislike about living in Britain?

3   Read Mary's interview with Pablo and answer the questions.

Mary: Where do you come from, Pablo?
Pablo: I come from Barcelona, Spain.
Mary: Why did you come to England?
Pablo: I wanted to study Computer Science at London University.
Mary: How long have you been here?
Pablo: Two years. I have just finished my second year at university.
Mary: Have you ever lived in a foreign country before?
Pablo: No, I haven't. I have visited other countries of course, but only for holidays. This is the first time I've ever lived in another country.
Mary: How are you getting on? Have you had problems with the language?
Pablo: Not really. My mother is English and we speak English and Spanish at home.
Mary: What do you like most about living in England?
Pablo: The people. I've made a lot of friends here.
Mary: What do you dislike about living here?
Pablo: The weather, of course! England is very cold and rainy. And the food at the university is awful. I've had some lovely English food in restaurants, though.
Mary: Are you going to stay here long?
Pablo: At least two more years, until I have completed my course.
Mary: What are you going to do after university? What are your ambitions?
Pablo: I'm going to set up my own business. I want to design and sell computer games.
Mary: Well, good luck Pablo. I hope you will succeed!

1   Where does Pablo come from?
2   What is he studying?
3   How long has Pablo been in England?
4   Has he ever lived in another country before?
5   Has he had any problems with the language?
6   What does he like most about living in England?
7   What does he dislike?
8   What is he going to do after university?

52

4 Match the words with their definitions.

1	course	a	dreams, wishes
2	getting on	b	establish
3	ambitions	c	set of lessons
4	succeed	d	managing
5	set up	e	achieve what you want

5 Read Pablo's interview again and fill in the table below.

NAME: *Pablo*
WHERE FROM: *Spain*
REASON FOR COMING: ....
....
HOW LONG IN ENGLAND: ....
LIVED IN OTHER COUNTRIES: ....
PROBLEMS WITH THE LANGUAGE: ....
....
LIKES MOST IN BRITAIN: ....
....
DISLIKES MOST IN BRITAIN: ....
....
FUTURE PLANS: ....
....

6 Fill in the correct question word(s).

1 "...*Where*... do you come from?" "Australia."
2 "....................... did you come to England?" "In 1996."
3 "............... did you come here?" "To find a better job."
4 "............................... have you been in Paris?" "For three years."
5 "............................. are you getting on with your new job?" "I have no problems at all."
6 "........... are you staying with?" "With my friend, Pam."
7 "........................... countries have you visited so far?" "France and Austria."
8 "......................... are you going to do after university?" "Set up my own restaurant."

7 Write questions to which the bold type words are the answers, as in the example.

1 *Where does Marco come from?*
Marco comes from **Italy**.
2 ....
He came here **six months ago**.

3 ....
I've visited **two** other European countries.
4 ....
Sally has known Todd **for ten years**.
5 ....
I go to my dance lessons **twice a week**.
6 ....
Nora is staying with **her Aunt Rosie**.

STUDY TIP

• We use the **past simple** for an action which happened in the **past** at a **specific** time. **Time words** used with the **past simple** are **yesterday, ago, last** (**week, month,** etc.), **when, how long ago**, etc.
• We use the **present perfect** for an action which **started** in the **past** and **continues** up to the **present**. **Time words** used with the **present perfect** are **for, since, yet, so far, How long, Since when**, etc.
  e.g. **When did you** come here? Two years **ago**.
  How long ago did you come here? Two years **ago**.
  How long have you been here? **For** two years.
  Since when have you been here? **Since** 1996.

8 Complete the questions with the *past simple* or the *present perfect*.

1 How long .... (**you/know**) your friend Sally?
2 When .... (**you/start**) driving lessons?
3 How long ago .... (**you/visit**) Austria?
4 When .... (**you/find**) a job?
5 Since when .... (**you/have**) your car?
6 How long ago .... (**you/move**) to York?
7 How long .... (**you/be**) a medical student?
8 How long .... (**you/be**) interested in computers?

9 Jasmin is talking to Mary Harris about her life in England. Read the text and put the verbs in brackets into the *past simple*, *present simple* or *present perfect*.

I **1)** .... **(come)** from Cairo, Egypt. I **2)** .... **(come)** to England last year to learn English.

I **3)** .... **(be)** a waitress in a restaurant in London, but sometimes I **4)** .... **(help)** with the cooking, too. I **5)** .... **(be)** at this restaurant for six months and I **6)** .... **(learn)** a lot about English food so far! I even **7)** .... **(make)** my own pudding for the first time last week!

I **8)** .... **(go)** to my English lessons three times a week. I **9)** .... **(meet)** some very nice people there. One of them **10)** .... **(invite)** me to his party two days ago. I really **11)** .... **(like)** my life in England and I **12)** .... **(not/have)** any problems, yet!

10 Read the text in Ex. 9 again and think of possible questions that Mary asked Jasmin, as in the example.

e.g. Where do you come from?

STUDY TIP

- We use **be going to** to talk about **future plans** or **ambitions**.
  *e.g. What **are** you **going to** do after university?*
  I'm going to set up my own business.

11 In pairs, ask and answer questions about Pablo's future plans, as in the example.

e.g. • *What/after university?*
  set up my own business
  A: What are you going to do after university?
  B: I'm going to set up my own business.

1 What/this weekend?
  study for my exams
2 What/during the summer holidays?
  visit my parents in Spain
3 What/while you're in Britain?
  travel around Scotland and Wales
4 What/in the next two years?
  find a job and study at the same time

12 Fill in the table below with the correct job from the list, as in the example.

mechanic, librarian, newsreader, secretary, teacher, chef

JOB	PLACE OF WORK	JOB DESCRIPTION
nurse	hospital	looks after sick people
....	office	types letters, answers telephone
....	library	checks books coming in and out
....	garage	services and mends cars
....	restaurant	prepares food for customers
....	school	gives lessons
....	TV studio	presents the news

Now, in pairs ask and answer questions, as in the example.

e.g. A: What do you do?
B: I'm a nurse.
A: Where do you work?
B: In a hospital.
A: What do you do when you're at work?
B: I look after sick people.

13 Mary is talking to Eva from Poland. First match the questions to the answers, then act out the interview.

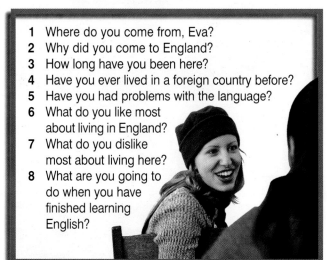

1 Where do you come from, Eva?
2 Why did you come to England?
3 How long have you been here?
4 Have you ever lived in a foreign country before?
5 Have you had problems with the language?
6 What do you like most about living in England?
7 What do you dislike most about living here?
8 What are you going to do when you have finished learning English?

| 1 | g | 2 | | 3 | | 4 | | 5 | | 6 | | 7 | | 8 | |

a Oh yes, but everyone at the factory helps me — especially with my pronunciation.
b Just a few months. I came here in March.
c Yes, I lived in France for a year.
d I wanted to learn English and experience the British way of life.
e I feel a bit lonely because I haven't made many friends yet.
f I'm going to train to become a nurse here.
g Poland.
h I love the shops and the night-life. The clubs are completely different here.

STUDY TIP

- We use various expressions to wish somebody **good luck** at the end of an interview.
  e.g. **Good luck, Pablo!**
  I hope you succeed!

14 Read the expressions below and tick the ones you can use at the end of an interview to wish somebody *good luck*.

1 I wish you every success! ☐
2 Have a nice day! ☐
3 I hope you get well soon! ☐
4 I wish you all the best! ☐
5 Be careful! ☐
6 Best of luck! ☐
7 Try hard! ☐
8 Congratulations! ☐

WRITING

TIP

When we **interview** someone who is living in a foreign country, we have to **ask about** the **place** he/she comes from, the **reason** for coming to the foreign country, the **problems** he/she possibly has, what he/she **likes** or **dislikes** about living there and his/her **future plans**. Always remember to **end the interview** with an expression wishing *good luck*.

15 Read Mary's notes below from her interview with Marco. Then, use the notes and the picture from the Photo File section to write out the complete interview for a magazine. You can start like this:

Mary: Marco. Thank you for talking to me today. Where do you come from?
Marco: I come from ....

Marco:
- From? — Rome, Italy
- Reason for coming? — learn about British cooking
- In England? — a year
- Lived in other countries? — No, visited France and Germany.
- Problems with language? — a few - names of dishes difficult
- Likes? — British humour, everyone polite
- Dislikes? — long working hours
- Future plans? — marry his British girlfriend Ann, open own restaurant

Mary!!

I ♥ Sports!

1 Name the sports in the pictures then read the sentences below and match them with the correct sport. Which of these are individual sports and which are team sports?

1 Scoring a goal makes you feel great.
2 Speeding down the snow slopes is very thrilling.
3 Catching the wave at the right moment is really enjoyable.
4 Being in the open air helps you relax.
5 Being in the water is fun.
6 Playing with a partner is exciting.

2 Read the article and list the points *for* and *against* swimming, then answer the questions that follow.

SWIMMING IS GREAT!

by Sheila Thompson, Toronto, Canada

Do you know the saying "like a duck to water"? That's me! Swimming is definitely my favourite sport. I love splashing around in the water, and I believe I'm not the only one.

Swimming is a very popular sport for various reasons. To start with, swimming is good exercise because it keeps you fit and healthy. It is good fun, too, as you can play lots of games in the water with your friends. Another good thing about swimming is that it is cheap. All you need is water and a swimming-costume!

On the other hand, learning to swim can be hard work because you must practise a lot. You need to spend lots of hours in the water before you learn to swim well. Also, swimming can sometimes be tiring. For example, professional swimmers need to push themselves to do their best. However, it is definitely worth it in the end.

All in all, although swimming can be hard work, I think it is a great way of exercising for everyone. It's an enjoyable sport for all the family, from children to grandparents.

1 Which paragraph mentions the points for swimming?
2 Why is swimming fun?
3 Which paragraph mentions the points against swimming?
4 Why can swimming be hard work?
5 What is the writer's opinion? In which paragraphs does she give her opinion?

3 Match the words from the text with their synonyms.

1 fit   **a** enjoyable
2 healthy   **b** train
3 fun   **c** in good shape
4 cheap   **d** certainly
5 practise   **e** well
6 definitely   **f** inexpensive

> Study these examples:
> We **go** fishing. We **play** tennis. We **do** weightlifting.

4 Fill in: *go, play* or *do*.

1 .... basketball   7 .... golf
2 .... running   8 .... windsurfing
3 .... karate   9 .... aerobics
4 .... swimming   10 .... baseball
5 .... football   11 .... cycling
6 .... gymnastics   12 .... scuba-diving

5 Put the verbs in brackets into the correct form: the *-ing* form or the *infinitive without to.*

1 People love .... **(go)** rafting. They find it thrilling.
2 Many people hate .... **(play)** golf because they find it boring.
3 You must .... **(practise)** every day to play tennis well.
4 Many people enjoy .... **(go)** scuba-diving because they find it interesting.
5 Karate can be a dangerous sport. For example, you may .... **(injure)** yourself quite badly.
6 Training to become a boxer can .... **(be)** very tiring because you need to practise a lot.

6 Look at the adjectives describing sports in the list below and decide which are positive and which are negative. Write P for positive and N for negative.

1 expensive ....N.........   7 exciting ....
2 easy ....   8 boring ....
3 hard ....   9 tiring ....
4 thrilling ....   10 healthy ....
5 popular ....   11 relaxing ....
6 dangerous ....   12 cruel ....

7 Match the adjectives which describe the points *for* with the reasons, then complete the sentences below.

cheap	you feel like you are flying over the waves
relaxing	you can play almost anywhere
thrilling	you don't need any special equipment
popular	you can forget about your problems

1 Football is very .... because ....
2 Golf is ....
3 Windsurfing is ....
4 Running is ....

8 Match the adjectives which describe the points *against* with the reasons, then complete the sentences.

expensive	you need to use a lot of energy
dangerous	the equipment costs a lot of money
tiring	it takes a long time to improve
hard	you might hurt yourself

1 Weightlifting is quite ....as............................
2 Basketball is sometimes ....
3 Skateboarding is often ....
4 Skiing is rather ....

I ♥ Sports!

UNIT 14

9 Join the sentences using *and, also, too, but, although* or *however*, as in the examples.

1 Cycling is cheap. It's relaxing. (similar ideas)
   e.g. *Cycling is cheap **and** relaxing.*
   *Cycling is cheap. It's **also** relaxing.*
   *Cycling is cheap. It's relaxing, **too**.*
2 Skiing is great. It's hard work. (opposing ideas)
   e.g. *Skiing is great, **but** it's hard work.*
   ***Although** skiing is great, it's hard work.*
   *Skiing is great. **However**, it's hard work.*
3 Tennis is fun. It's popular.
4 Skateboarding is tiring. It makes you feel energetic.
5 Football is a very popular sport. It can be dangerous.
6 Ice-skating is a difficult sport. It's tiring.
7 Car racing is an expensive sport. It's thrilling.
8 Scuba-diving is very interesting. It keeps you fit.
9 Fishing is cheap. It's relaxing.
10 Water polo is an exciting sport. It's fun.

10 Look at the pictures and talk about the points *for* and *against* each sport using *and, also, too, but, although* and *however*.
Adjectives to use: *popular, dangerous, thrilling, enjoyable, exciting, great, energetic, interesting, tiring, exhausting, relaxing,* etc.
Expressions to use: *I think ... , I believe ... , In my opinion ... ,* etc.

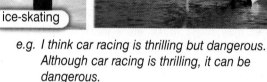

car racing sailing water-skiing ice-skating

e.g. *I think car racing is thrilling but dangerous.*
Although car racing is thrilling, it can be dangerous.

11 Read the text and correct the underlined mistakes. Some lines contain no mistakes.

Skiing is the sport I like ~~better~~. I live in a	**a** ....best....
small village in the mountains <u>which</u> there	**b** ....
is a lot of snow <u>but</u> I can ski every day.	**c** ....
Skiing is great fun <u>to</u> people who enjoy	**d** ....
<u>to be</u> outdoors. It's also a very thrilling	**e** ....
sport. Speeding down the slopes of the	**f** ....
mountains makes you <u>feeling</u> like a bird.	**g** ....
<u>Other</u> good thing about skiing is that it	**h** ....
<u>help</u> you relax. Being out in the fresh	**i** ....
air makes you <u>to</u> forget your problems.	**j** ....
However, learning to ski can sometimes	**k** ....
be dangerous as you <u>must</u> hurt yourself.	**l** ....
Sometimes it is also difficult and	**m** ....
tiring because you need a <u>lots</u> of time	**n** ....
to practise. To sum up, although skiing	**o** ....
can sometimes <u>is</u> difficult, I think	**p** ....
it's <u>a</u> excellent way to exercise.	**q** ....

12 Read the article below and fill in the missing topic sentences. Then, list the points *for* and *against* rock-climbing. Finally, answer the questions.

Topic Sentences

a On the other hand, rock-climbing can sometimes be dangerous.

b Rock-climbing is my favourite sport.

c In conclusion, I believe that, although rock-climbing can be dangerous, it is a fantastic sport.

d There are several reasons why rock-climbing is such a popular sport.

1 There is nothing I like better than being outdoors, standing high up on a mountain and looking down at the rest of the world.

2 To start with, it is very exciting because you can explore many interesting places. It is also good exercise, as it helps you keep fit and healthy. It's relaxing, too! Being out in the fresh air can help you forget your everyday problems.

3 For example, you have to be very careful and well-trained to avoid having an accident. It is also rather expensive, as the equipment costs quite a lot of money.

4 It is the perfect way to exercise and travel around the countryside at the same time. Try it and see for yourself!

points for	*points against*
....	....
....	....
....	....
....	....

1 Which paragraph includes the points **for** rock-climbing?

2 Which paragraph includes the points **against** rock-climbing?

3 In which paragraphs does the writer give his opinion?

4 Underline the words the writer used to link the points **for/against** rock-climbing.

5 Which words can be replaced by **all in all/to sum up**?

WRITING

TIP

Before you write an **article expressing your opinion about a sport** you like, always make a list of **the points for** and **against** the sport. **In the first paragraph**, say what your favourite sport is and why you like it. **In the second paragraph**, write the points **for** the sport with reasons. **In the third paragraph**, write the points **against** the sport with reasons. Start the **last paragraph** with: In conclusion, All in all, To sum up. In the last paragraph, give your opinion. Use expressions such as: I think ..., I believe ..., In my opinion ... etc. Use **linking words** (and, so, too, but, although, however, etc) to link **similar** or **opposing** ideas.

13 Use the plan below and choose a sport from the Photo File section to write *an article for your school magazine about the sport you like most.*

Plan

Paragraph 1: say what your favourite sport is and why you like it
↓

Paragraph 2: write the positive points about the sport (give reasons)
↓

Paragraph 3: write the negative points about the sport (give reasons)
↓

Paragraph 4: give your opinion and reason

UNIT 15

All about Disney!

1 Look at the pictures. Who are these people?

2 Match the following descriptions to the pictures.

1 A famous novelist who wrote many murder mysteries.
2 A famous singer who is known as the *King of Rock 'n' Roll*.
3 A famous explorer who opened up a whole new underwater world to everyone.
4 A famous animator who created lovable cartoon characters such as *Mickey Mouse* and *Donald Duck*.

3 Read Walt Disney's biography and answer the questions.

Walt Disney is a well-known name all over the world. He was the famous animator who created characters such as *Mickey Mouse* and *Donald Duck*. Disney's films have entertained millions of people over the years and are still popular today.

Walter Elias Disney was born in Chicago on December 5th, 1901. He was one of five children and grew up on a farm in Missouri. Many of his first drawings as a child were of farm animals. At the age of sixteen, Disney returned to Chicago where he studied art at McKinley High School.

In 1920 he joined the Kansas City Ad Company, where he made cartoon advertisements. Disney's ambition, though, was to make films, so in 1923 he decided to go to Hollywood. Walt and his brother Roy set up their own small company in a small office there. Disney got married to Lillian Bounds on July 13th, 1925. They had two daughters, Diane and Sharon. In 1928, he created *Mickey Mouse*, his most famous cartoon character. That was the start of Disney's amazing success. His company grew and he won many awards for his films, which include *Snow White and the Seven Dwarfs*, *Bambi* and *Pinocchio*. His greatest creation, however, was Disneyland, which opened in 1955 in California.

Walt Disney died at the age of 65 on December 15th, 1966. Sadly, he didn't live to see the opening of the world-famous Disney World in Florida, in 1971. His dreams live on, though, and people can share them by watching his films and going to his amusement parks.

1 Who was Walt Disney?
2 Where was he born?
3 When was he born?
4 Where did he grow up?
5 What were his first drawings of?
6 What did he study at high school?
7 What did he do in 1920?
8 Where did he start a business with his brother?
9 Who did he marry?
10 What are some of his famous films?
11 What happened in 1955?
12 When did Disney die?

4 Find the following words in the text, underline and explain them. Then use the words to complete the sentences below.

animator, awards, creation, ambition, amusement park

1 The most famous .... in the world is Disney World in Florida.
2 Disney's first job as a(n) .... was with the Kansas City Ad Company.
3 *Dumbo the Elephant* was a(n) .... of Walt Disney.
4 Disney's films were very popular and he won many .... for them.
5 As a young boy, Disney's .... was to make films and cartoons.

5 Read the text again and find the information to fill in the table below.

1901	Disney was born on December 5th in Chicago.
AT THE AGE OF 16	....
1920	....
1923	....
JULY 13TH, 1925	....
1928	....
1955	....
DECEMBER 15TH, 1966	....

Use the information from the table above, and talk about the most important events in Disney's life.

STUDY TIP

• We often use the **past simple** of the **passive voice** (was, were + past participle) in **biographies**.
e.g. *Walter Elias Disney **was born** in 1901.*

6 Fill in the sentences below with the correct form of the verbs in brackets, as in the example.

1 J. F. Kennedy *was shot* **(shoot)** in Dallas.

2 *Hamlet* .... **(write)** by Shakespeare.

3 Marilyn Monroe's last film .... **(make)** in 1960.

4 Robert Louis Stevenson .... **(bring up)** in Scotland.

5 Television .... **(invent)** by John Logi Baird.

6 The *Little Tramp* .... **(create)** by Charlie Chaplin.

STUDY TIP

• We often use **prepositions of place** and **prepositions of time** when we write biographies.
e.g. *Disney was born **on** December 5th, 1901.*
*He was born **in** Chicago.*
***At** the age of sixteen, he returned to Chicago.*
*He joined the Kansas City Ad Company **in** 1920.*

7 Fill in the gaps with the correct prepositions: *in, on* or *at.*

Agatha Christie was born **1)** *on* September 15th, 1890. She was born **2)** .... Devon, England. She was educated **3)** .... home by her mother. **4)** .... 1914 she married Archibald Christie. Her first novel was published **5)** .... 1920, when she introduced Hercule Poirot, the famous detective. Her most famous books include *Death* **6)** .... *the Nile* and *Murder* **7)** .... *the Orient Express*. One of her plays, *The Mousetrap*, played **8)** .... the Ambassador Theatre for twenty-one years. She divorced Archibald and married Sir Max Mallowan, an archaeologist, **9)** .... 1930. Agatha Christie died **10)** .... January 12th, 1976 **11)** .... the age of eighty-five.

All about Disney!

STUDY TIP

- We can **join two sentences** by using **relative pronouns** or **adverbs** (who, which, where, etc). We use **who** for people, **which** for objects and **where** for places.

  e.g. *He was the famous animator. He created characters such as Mickey Mouse and Donald Duck.*
  *He was the famous animator **who** created characters such as Mickey Mouse and Donald Duck.*

8 Join the sentences below with *who, which* or *where*, as in the example.

e.g. *Walt Disney joined the Kansas City Ad Company. He made cartoons there.*
*Walt Disney joined the Kansas City Ad Company **where** he made cartoons.*

1 Charlie Chaplin's first film was *Making a Living*. It was a great success.
2 Picasso was a famous artist. He painted *Guernica*.
3 In November 1963 J. F. Kennedy travelled to Dallas. He was shot there by Lee Harvey Oswald.
4 Rudolf Nureyev danced in *Romeo and Juliet*. It was performed in London.
5 Hitchcock directed *Psycho*. It became one of the most famous thrillers in history.
6 Wilbur and Orville Wright were brothers. They designed the first aeroplane.

9 Read Marilyn Monroe's biography and fill in the gaps with a verb from the list in the correct tense.

change, grow up, star, work, make, become, die, join, be, spend, meet, get

Even today, over thirty years after her death, people are still trying to copy Marilyn Monroe's style. She **1)** .... famous in the 1950's and is probably this century's best-known blonde.

Norma Jean Baker (Marilyn) **2)** .... born on June 1st, 1926. She **3)** .... in Los Angeles and **4)** .... some time at the Los Angeles Orphans' Home. At the age of sixteen she **5)** .... Jim Dougherty and they **6)** .... married. For a while she **7)** .... in a factory, packing parachutes for the U.S. Army.

In 1946 she **8)** .... Fox Studios where she **9)** .... her name to Marilyn Monroe. In the same year she **10)** .... in her first film *Scudda-Hoo! Scudda-Hay!* One of her most famous films, however, is *Gentlemen Prefer Blondes* which she **11)** .... in 1952.

Marilyn **12)** .... alone at home on August 5th, 1962. She was just 36 years old. The woman is gone, but the legend lives on.

10 Look at the table below and, in pairs, ask and answer questions about Elvis Presley, as in the example. Use question words such as *what, where, who, when,* etc.

JANUARY 8TH, 1935	born in Tupelo, Mississippi
AT THE AGE OF 11	first played guitar
1948	moved to Memphis, Tennessee
AS A YOUNG MAN	worked as a truck driver
1956	first hit record *Heartbreak Hotel*
1958	joined the U.S. Army and went to Germany
1960	returned to U.S. with 16-year-old Priscilla Beaulieu
JANUARY 5TH, 1967	married Priscilla
1971	received Grammy Award
AUGUST 16TH, 1977	died at the age of 42 of heart failure

e.g. A: When was Elvis Presley born?
B: He was born on January 8th, 1935.
A: Where was he born?
B: He was born ...

62

WRITING

TIP

When we write a **biography**, we divide it into **four paragraphs**. In the **first paragraph**, we say who the **person** is and what he/she is **famous** for. In the **second paragraph**, we give **information** about his/her **early life** (when/where born, education, etc). In the **third paragraph**, we give **information** about his/her life as an **adult** (marriage, achievements, etc). In the **fourth paragraph**, we write about his/her **death** and how **people feel about him/her**. We use the past simple when we write biographies about people who have died.

11 Look at the table about Jacques-Yves Cousteau and answer the questions.

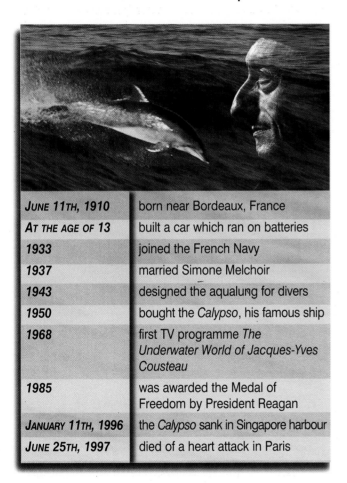

JUNE 11TH, 1910	born near Bordeaux, France
AT THE AGE OF 13	built a car which ran on batteries
1933	joined the French Navy
1937	married Simone Melchoir
1943	designed the aqualung for divers
1950	bought the *Calypso*, his famous ship
1968	first TV programme *The Underwater World of Jacques-Yves Cousteau*
1985	was awarded the Medal of Freedom by President Reagan
JANUARY 11TH, 1996	the *Calypso* sank in Singapore harbour
JUNE 25TH, 1997	died of a heart attack in Paris

1 When and where was Jacques-Yves Cousteau born?
2 What did Jacques-Yves Cousteau do as young boy?
3 What did he do in 1933?
4 Who did he marry?
5 What did he design for divers?

6 When did he buy the *Calypso*?
7 What was his first TV programme called?
8 What happened in 1985?
9 Where and when did the *Calypso* sink?
10 When and where did Jacques-Yves Cousteau die?
11 What did he die of?

12 Read the following sentences about Cousteau's life and say which paragraph they belong to.

a In his early teens Cousteau became bored with school but he was very interested in machines and films.
b He is dead but his message to the world lives on: "The planet belongs to all of us and it's our duty to protect it!"
c In 1974, Cousteau started the Cousteau Society to protect ocean life.
d Jacques-Yves Cousteau was the man who brought the mysteries of the ocean into millions of homes with his documentaries.

paragraph 1 .... paragraph 3 ....
paragraph 2 .... paragraph 4 ....

13 Use the information from Exs. 11 and 12, the picture from the Photo File section and the plan below to write a biography about Jacques-Yves Cousteau.

Plan

Paragraph 1:
• say who the person is
• say what he is famous for

Paragraph 2:
• give information about his life as a young man (when/where born, education, etc)

Paragraph 3:
• give information about his life as an adult (marriage, achievements, etc)

Paragraph 4:
• write about his death
• how people feel about him

PHOTO FILE SECTION

**(The pictures in this section are to be
cut out and used to decorate your writing projects in
Units 3, 6, 8, 11, 13, 14 and 15.)**

UNIT 3

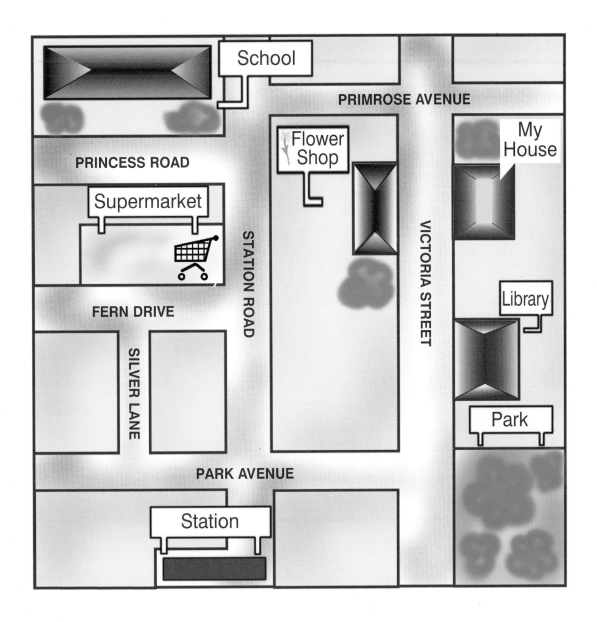